JAMES CUTLER

CONTEMPORARY
WORLD
ARCHITECTS

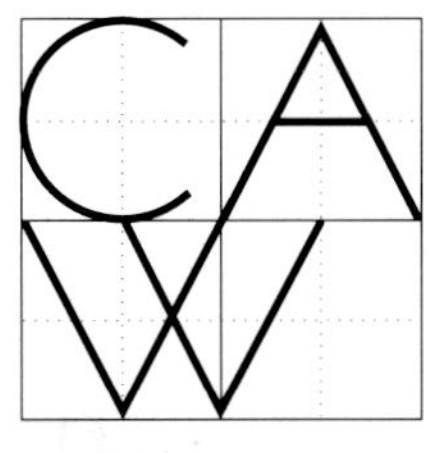

JAMES CUTLER

Foreword by
Peter Bohlin

Introduction by
James Wines

Text by
Theresa Morrow

Concept and Design by
Lucas H. Guerra
Oscar Riera Ojeda

ROCKPORT PUBLISHERS
GLOUCESTER, MASSACHUSETTS

First published in the United States of America by:
Rockport Publishers, Inc.
146 Granite Street
Rockport, Massachusetts 01966
Telephone: (508) 546-9590
Fax: (508) 546-7141

Distributed to the book trade and art trade in the United States of America by
North Light Books,an imprint of
F & W Publications
1507 Dana Avenue
Cincinnati, Ohio 45207
Telephone: (800) 289-0963

Distribution by:
Rockport Publishers, Inc.
Rockport, Massachusetts 01966

ISBN 1-56496-341-1

10 9 8 7

Printed in China

Cover Photograph: Virginia Merrill Bloedel Education Center by Art Grice
Back Cover Photographs: (Top) Guest House by Art Grice, (Bottom) Wright Guest House by Art Grice
Back Flap Photograph: James Cutler by Art Grice
Pages 1-3 Photograph: Guest House by Karl A. Backus

Graphic Design: Lucas H. Guerra / Oscar Riera Ojeda
Connexus Visual Communication / Boston
Layout: Oscar Riera Ojeda
Editor: Don Fluckinger

CONTENTS

Foreword

BY PETER BOHLIN

Jim and I have been friends for most of our lives. He was raised in Pennsylvania's anthracite coal region with its great culm banks and strippings where man tore coal from the earth. He worked in our practice while he attended Penn, building models during holidays and vacations.

Jim was drawn to the University of Pennsylvania by Loren Eisely, where he found Lou Kahn. As with Kahn, at the root of Jim's architecture are his values, his deeply held beliefs, the sanctity of the natural world, our need to value it, to find a gentle relationship to it, to give to it as well as take from it. . . and to feel loss and sadness when we inevitably take. Soon after graduating from Penn he moved from the East to the Pacific Northwest, with its forests and the sea.

One can often see the roots of Jim's plans in Kahn's studio—their simplicity and seeming inevitability—but also growing from the North- west, an American architecture of the Pacific Rim. Jim is horrified by man's destruction of the natural world. Following the example of the Native Americans, he believes that if trees are cut, one should honor them by using them wisely and frugally, thereby expressing their nature.

There has been a progression in Jim's architecture—it has become more personal, less derivative, much more poignant. An architecture that is both spare and touching, it reveals the essence of each particular circumstance.

The juxtaposition of wood and concrete overlaid with the encroaching vegetation is an attempt to create an architecture that is a responsive servant of nature—not the other way around.

Introduction

BY JAMES WINES

James Cutler is one of the most distinguished members of a new generation of architects who have embraced the environmental revolution and created an original body of work to reflect this commitment. He is also a designer who has honored and learned from the heritage of Frank Lloyd Wright, and has given a distinctly contemporary sensibility to this master's contributions to contextual architecture. At the same time, from a technical perspective, Cutler's work includes an ecological awareness that was not known in Wright's era.

Frank Lloyd Wright was clearly this century's leading prophet of environmental design. Through his philosophy of organic architecture and the interpretation of building as an extension of site, he was a seminal influence on today's relationship between construction and nature. When the Wright show at the Museum of Modern Art closed its doors in 1994, the world community of "green design" advocates assumed this awesome exhibition would have a major impact on architects. To the contrary, while the MOMA exhibit did generate critical discussion of his environmental contributions, the mainstream of the architecture profession seems to have virtually ignored this aspect of his work and its relevance to our emerging Age of Ecology.

This rejection is nothing new. In the 1930s, Wright's unique American contextualism and earth-centered ideas were eclipsed by the more fashionably seductive imagery of the Machine Age. Since then, most of his organic architecture innovations have tended to be misunderstood, overlooked, or dismissed by orthodox Modernists as evidence of Wright's regressive tendency to favor nineteenth-century arcadias over technological futures. To a great extent, this misguided interpretation of Wright still prevails—particularly now, when everything he stood for can be seen as threatening to the currently entrenched architectural styles of high-tech, neo-Constructivism, and late Modernism.

It must be noted that James Cutler's connection to Wright should not be confused with a cottage industry of cloying clichés that have grown out of what might be called the "Falling Water rustic" syndrome; (one of its primary generators being the subjugating influence still wielded by the master's posthumous design mortuary at Taliesin West). The point is mentioned here because this kind of derivative Wrightian baggage has frequently been a prime target for disdain by the progressive architectural establishment and has created a confusion of values where any hint of natural materials or leafy terraces in a building can be seen as the basis for mainstream rejection. To some extent the work of James Cutler has not been given due recognition, based on a blind appreciation of this critical premise. In his case, however, it only demonstrates the apprehension gnawing at the high-tech design practitioners, as they face the realization that architects of Cutler's formidable talent embrace a set of environmentally responsible values that may endanger their entire stylistic investment. As a footnote it is amusing to observe that, while the current neo-Constructivist camp considers contextualism, plant life, and stone walls as evidence of the regressively picturesque, their own catalog of materials and imagery is identified with a reactionary celebration of structural technology—that ultimate example of a nostalgic 1920s iconography.

As the millennium approaches, Wright's vision of architecture as a responsive servant of nature seems destined to be resurrected as one of the building art's most relevant and influential legacies. All of the stylistic diversions that distracted from the importance of his approach have been rooted in this century's earlier Age of Industry and Technology—an influence now more than ninety years old and the equivalent (in terms of its pervasive

conventions) of a 1990s version of the 1890s Beaux Arts academy. Today, the focus on ecology has raised nagging doubts concerning the wisdom of maintaining this tradition. As an alternative for the future, the environmental initiative seems to be the logical choice. It is a source of ideas and imagery that may change architecture more dramatically in the next two decades than it has changed during the past hundred years.

A rapidly growing (but still very small) community of architects has begun to see the urgency of its role in reversing the wasteful and irresponsible course of building construction and land use during the last few decades. In addition, an ecological awareness has already shaped many aspects of civic standards, politics, economics, industry, and the sciences. Witness, for example, the recent convulsions of environmental policy reversal in Washington. Ever since right-wing politicians focused on recent statistical reports announcing that seventy-five percent of American citizens consider the environment a top priority in progressive legislation, conservative bureaucrats have been stumbling over themselves to take advantage of photo ops where they can wax green against backgrounds of verdant landscape and petting zoos. On the other hand, it is a sad reality that one of the most regressive professions (in terms of its resistance to the ecological message) is the architectural establishment. Granted, there is considerable lip service paid to the sustainability issue in professional design journals and at American Institute of Architects (AIA) conferences; but the fact remains that more than ninety percent of edifices erected during the past few years have been the same blast-out-a-hole-and-build intrusions that have fouled the land surface and wasted precious resources for most of this century.

James Cutler is one of those rare contemporary architects who has converted environmental technology, an ecologically responsible choice of materials, and a strong earth consciousness into art. In contrast to his approach, it is typical today to visit one of the rare examples of well-intentioned "green" architecture, be handed a written text at the door describing the structure's environmental virtues; but then find that the architect's choice of design imagery perpetuates the same ubiquitous kit of parts characteristic of any routine building. The intentions are admirable; but the results are boring. In Cutler's work, on the other hand, the site area, regional topography, local vegetation, and the "psychology of situation" become intrinsic parts of his aesthetic decisions. With regard to this psychological element, it refers to his ability to connect to an ambient sensibility representative of a widely held consensus (or tap into what Jung called "a collective unconscious") that gives any art form its communicative impact and sense of relevance. In our time, this unifying sensibility has been defined by our acknowledgment that, if we are to survive as a species, the damage wrought by global industrialization must be reversed.

(Above) A typical example of James Cutler's recycling of a building: In the Parker Residence, originally a fishnet drying shed, the architect kept the original warehouse features. The industrial window patterns are also reflected in the open plan.

While Cutler's work incorporates a form of construction technology that clearly identifies him as an architect of the 1990s, he does not celebrate industrial imagery the way, for example, that the buildings of Rem Koolhaas, Jean Nouvel, Richard Rogers, Renzo Piano, Norman Foster and a host of other prominent designers harken back to Machine Age sources. Cutler's buildings, like Wright's, grow out of complex architectural investigations. They are based on an understanding of the unique qualities of each situation, rather than an adherence to some prescriptive set of forms endorsed by a fashionable "in" movement or the comfortable reassurances of an easily accessible design vocabulary.

Cutler has described his work as "a narrative of our relationship to our environment." In this respect—as in the design of the Bridge House on Bainbridge Island, Washington—he has constructed the building with careful respect to the terrain and vegetation. The residence sits on a masonry truss that bridges a local stream, and creates the effect of architecture as a floating and intrinsic presence among the trees. This integrated concept is further enhanced by textures and rhythms embodied in structural elements that seem to have grown naturally out of the surroundings. Although the actual building has a low and horizontal elevation—with shingled walls and a pitched metal roof—its vertical timber elements are orchestrated in such a way that they seem to be a mutable and evolutionary extension of the forest's growing cycle.

Antonio Gaudi, the great Catalan architect, explored the concept of structure itself as both a metaphor and engineered equivalent for nature's systems of growth. His famous towers, facades, and viaducts served as narrative descriptions of this process; but they were conceived primarily for an urban situation. James Cutler's work, on the other hand, is frequently located in the more accommodating natural environment of the Pacific Northwest. His philosophical principles, however, have parallels with Gaudi's. Cutler's buildings do not share the Spanish master's vision of Gothic grandeur—given their usually restricted budgets and rural sites—but, the intention to build ideas out of nature's integrated systems demonstrates a similar objective. Unlike Wright, who built edifices as a sculptural counterpoint to nature and Gaudi, who built architecture as nature's spiritual embodiment, James Cutler builds to establish an ongoing dialogue with the unique qualities of the land. If Wright and Gaudi can be described as designers of environmental monuments, then Cutler is a builder of modest tree houses. His works are quiet, unobtrusive, and ecologically responsive—but their message is the wave of the future.

Crumbling concrete walls in Holden Village (in the North Cascades) contrast with the surrounding natural beauty. This scene provided the design inspiration for the Guest House (see photo, page 56), where the interior walls take on the same crumbling appearance.

Nature takes its course: (Top) In the Guest House, stone plinths support the building. (Center) The Bridge House literally rests on a bridge, leaving a natural ravine and seasonal stream minimally disturbed. Floating over a ravine, the Houdek/Pope Residence (Bottom) is connected to the land with a minimal footprint.

Boxes ▶

Daubenberger Residence

PORT TOWNSEND, WASHINGTON

Built in 1974 on top of an abandoned concrete bunker—the 5-acre (2-hectare) property formerly was used for a government fort, from which the remains of several gun emplacements were left behind—the 950-square-foot (85.5-square-meter) Daubenberger Residence represents an early effort to master the materials of the Northwest. Though formally mannered after Robert Venturi's Trubek and Wislocki Houses on Nantucket Island, the plan displays a budding comprehension of the "institution" of family, while retaining a simple, ordered, and symmetrical plan.

To minimize the impact of the building, the residence was set on existing concrete of the gun emplacements. The wood-frame building is sided and roofed in native red cedar, trimmed with Douglas fir. In order to flood the building with light and to open it up to the surrounding views of the straits of Juan de Fuca and the Olympic Mountains, the living spaces are glazed on three sides.

In keeping with the Victorian context of nearby Port Townsend, the 30-foot-high house stretches four levels, in vertical counterpoint to the surrounding alfalfa fields. The core "servant" spaces are placed as a screen on the non-view road access side of the building in order to protect the privacy of the owners without taking away from the predominant views.

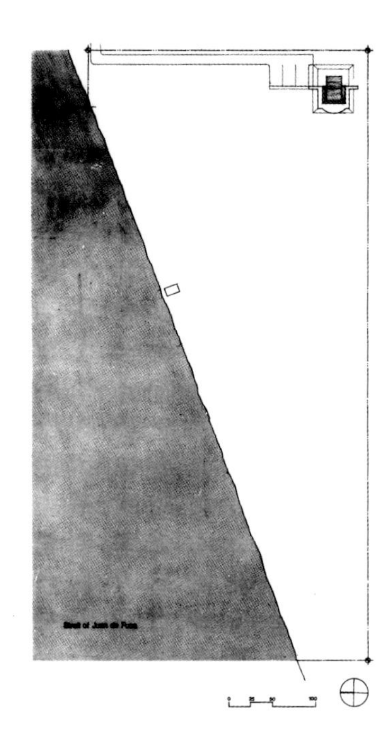

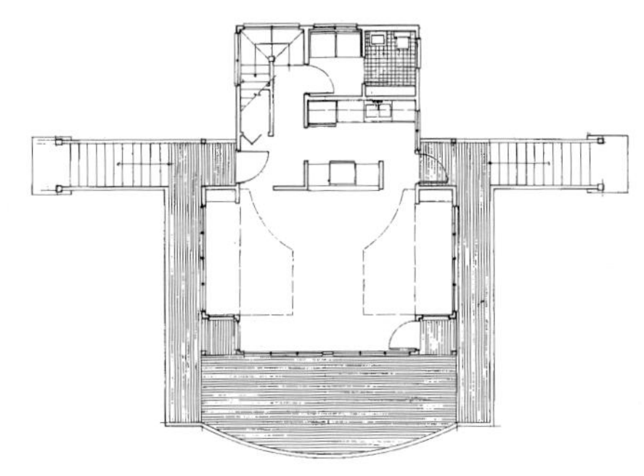

FIRST FLOOR PLAN

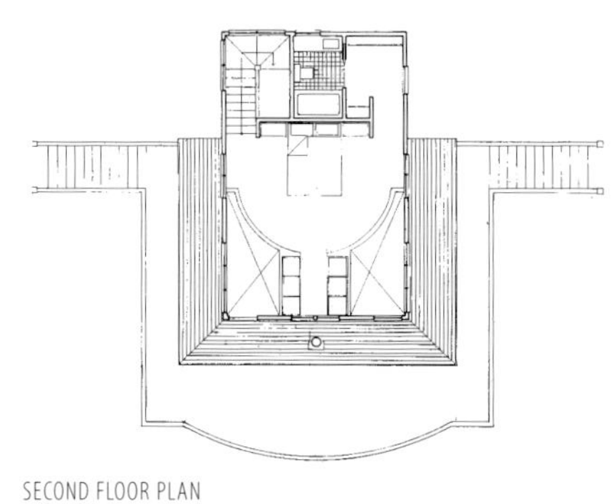

SECOND FLOOR PLAN

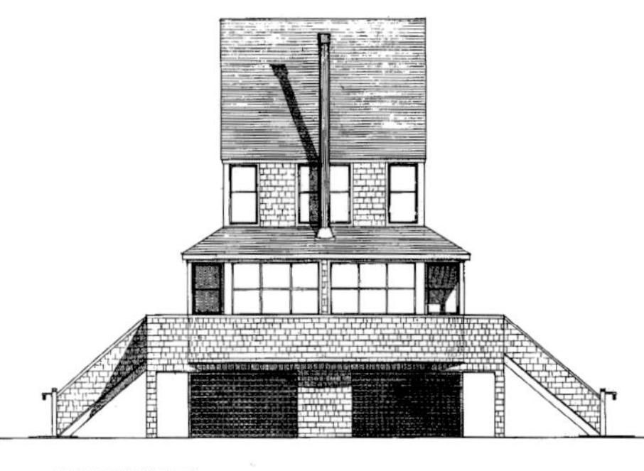

WEST ELEVATION

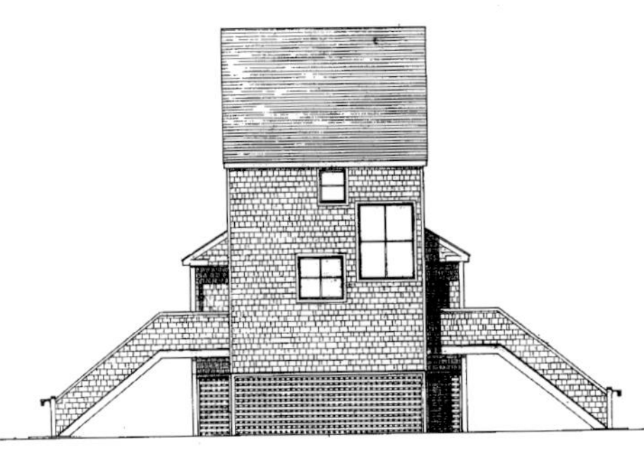

EAST ELEVATION

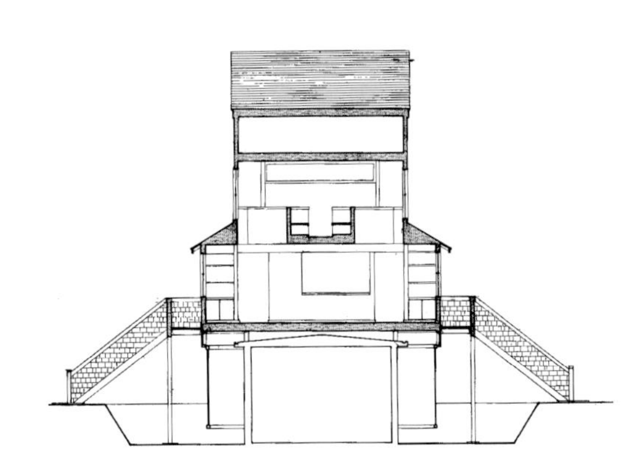

NORTH ELEVATION

SOUTH ELEVATION

The tie to the Northwest surroundings is evident in the cedar shingle exterior and Shingle-style design. The living room connects with the surrounding landscape. An open bedroom allows for more light in the living room, visually enlarging the the small house.

Parker Residence

BAINBRIDGE ISLAND, WASHINGTON

Built inside the shell of a 1920s net-drying shed, this Shingle-style building evolved to visually address its industrial harbor context. Because the building was positioned at the toe of a 12-foot (4-meter) embankment, the entry needed to be located on the second level, while the living (public) level logically should have been placed at dock level. The architects felt that the stair from the entry to the living level needed to be generous enough to invite guests down while still having enough of a sense of enclosure at the entry level so that the stair didn't feel precipitous. To achieve this, the stair was narrowed at the top and flared at the bottom.

The variety of natural woods—fir floors, hemlock walls, fir cabinetry, cedar shingle walls and roof—is worked to highlight how they are joined together in the construction process. The interior of the building is structured to carry the second floor while still keeping a vestige of the initial shed volume. Separating the bedroom spaces from the entry by two steps up allows privacy for those rooms, yet leaves them open to the volume. The building is heated by a low-temperature, salt-water-to-fresh-water heat pump that minimizes energy consumption.

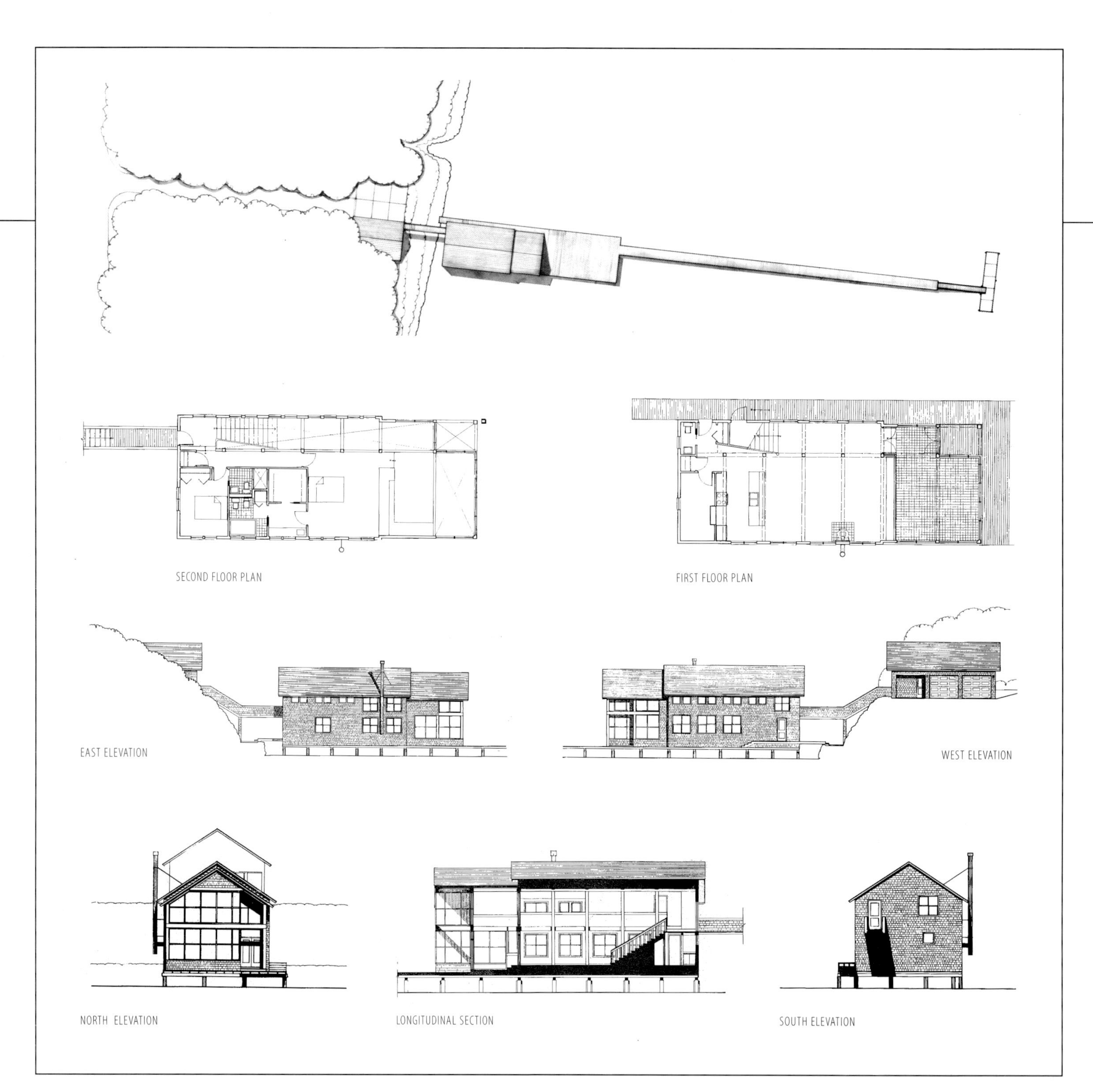
SECOND FLOOR PLAN
FIRST FLOOR PLAN
EAST ELEVATION
WEST ELEVATION
NORTH ELEVATION
LONGITUDINAL SECTION
SOUTH ELEVATION

The functional spaces of the house run lengthwise, with a two-story sun room replacing the area where fishnets once hung to dry. Carefully placed clerestories let in light, and a former storage loft upstairs is transformed into bedrooms, bathrooms, and a den. The slightly twisted stairway at the entrance is an invitation to guests to enter the lower living area of the house, while still giving a sense of enclosure to the entry.

Catskills Residence

LEW BEACH, NEW YORK

Stone and wood combine in this project—a residence that resembles an Adirondack hunting lodge—to symbolize both the permanence and decay that come with the passage of time. Preliminary surveys of the land for this residence in the Catskills Mountains led to the discovery of the ruins of old fieldstone farm walls crisscrossing the area. The architect used these existing features of the land to place the residence on a bluestone platform that is regular to the grid of the existing walls. Though the stone platform is on a north/south grid marked by one of the existing farm walls, the house is twisted on that grid toward the view. The building appears as an airy pavilion on a heavy base.

To allow the house to unfold and open into the landscape, full-height windows turn the living room into a sun room in winter and a screened-in porch in summer. The roof overhang deflects direct sunlight.

The "totemic" building accommodates the fly fishing owner's love of nature. It also acknowledges the Native American respect for life in nature, which includes the taking of life to enable others to live. Motifs of local wildlife accent light fixtures, the stairway and even the steel connectors.

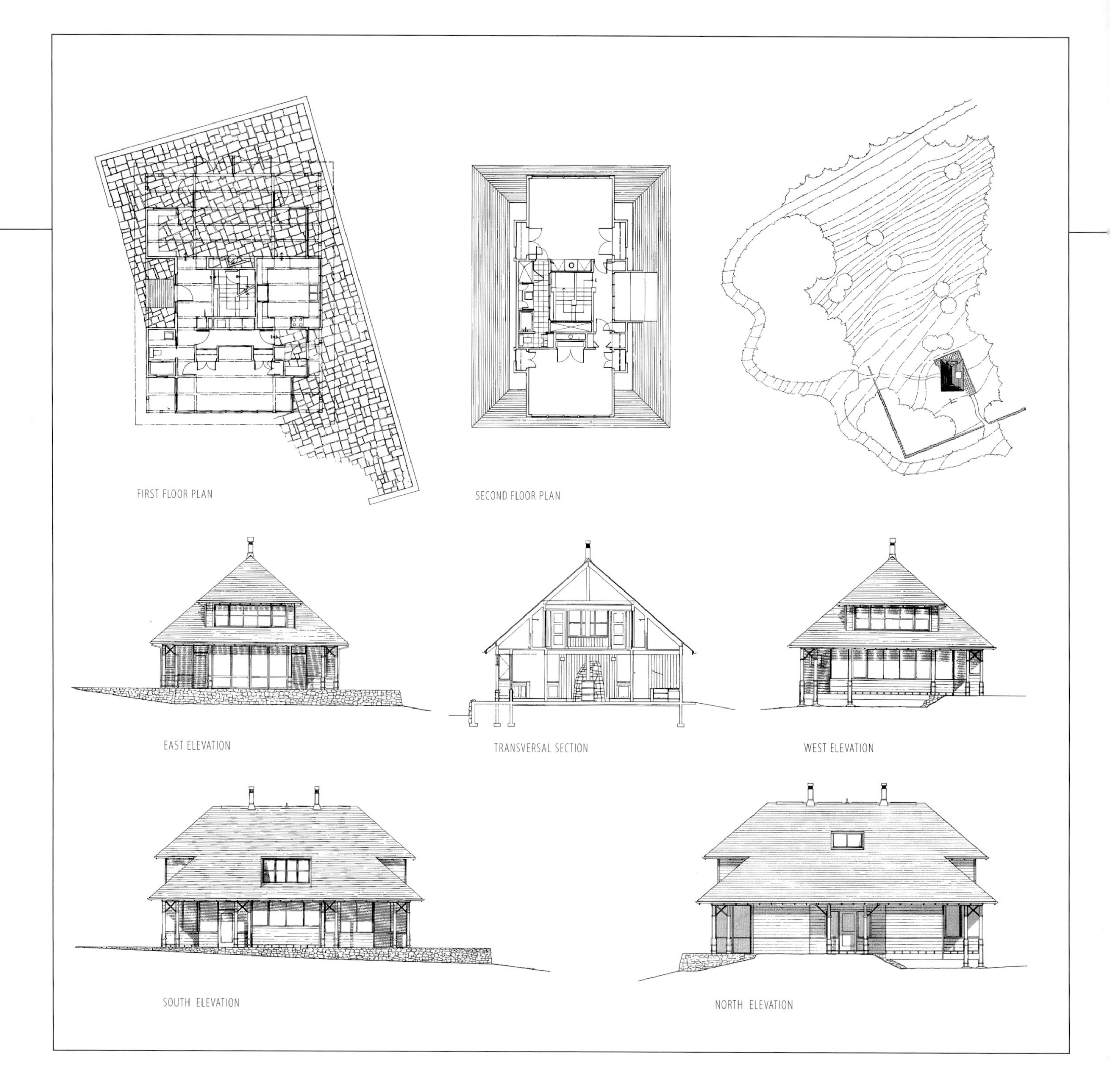
FIRST FLOOR PLAN
SECOND FLOOR PLAN
EAST ELEVATION
TRANSVERSAL SECTION
WEST ELEVATION
SOUTH ELEVATION
NORTH ELEVATION

In the Catskills Residence, stone and wood combine to symbolize both permanence and decay. The design resembles that of an Adirondack hunting lodge: white pine predominates inside, with cherry wood used in the kitchen. A white-pigmented stain brightens the pine walls and contrasts with darker millwork; (Center) custom casements in the living area allow for removable screens to turn the space into a screened porch. (Top) Jigsawed cutouts of local trout decorate the central staircase.

The Bridge House

BAINBRIDGE ISLAND, WASHINGTON

Environmental concerns came first in this residence, which spans a seasonal stream on a heavily wooded parcel of land on Bainbridge Island, Washington. Initially, the land was thought to be unbuildable, its half-acre bisected by a ravine and stream. A potential client had already received a permit to culvert the stream and build a colonial residence, but after some discussion was convinced to give up such an environmentally destructive scheme.

Built over the stream, the "speculative" Bridge House house was intended to set an example for a more sensitive response to the land. Beyond limiting the building's footprint, an effort was made to carefully design the process of construction so that "collateral" damage to the land was limited. The result can be seen in the photo of the west elevation (page 30), taken three weeks before the completion of construction.

The building itself spans 42 feet (13 meters) across the stream between its concrete block abutments. All the footings were hand-dug and the spanning floor deck was used as a staging area. In an effort to create a non-toxic structure, the building was built "formaldehyde-free," with no plywood or toxic paints.

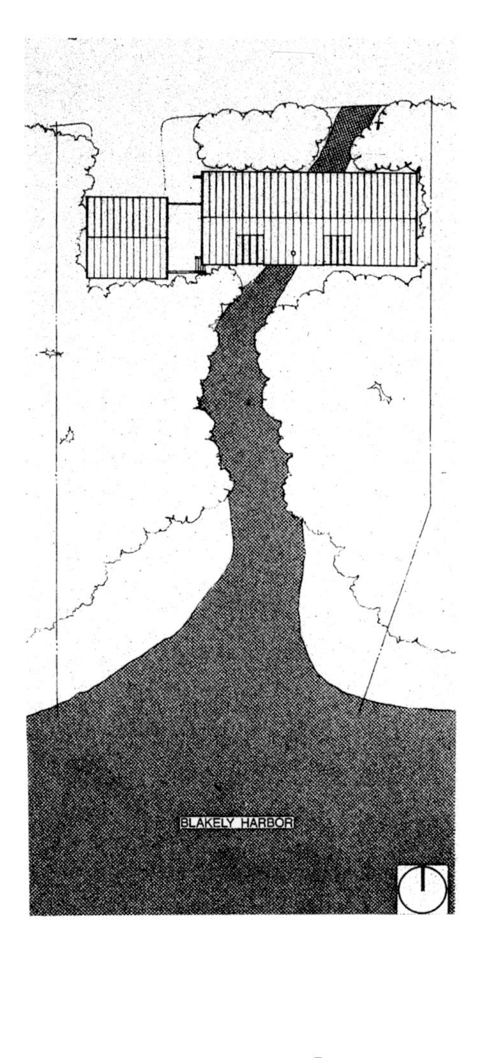

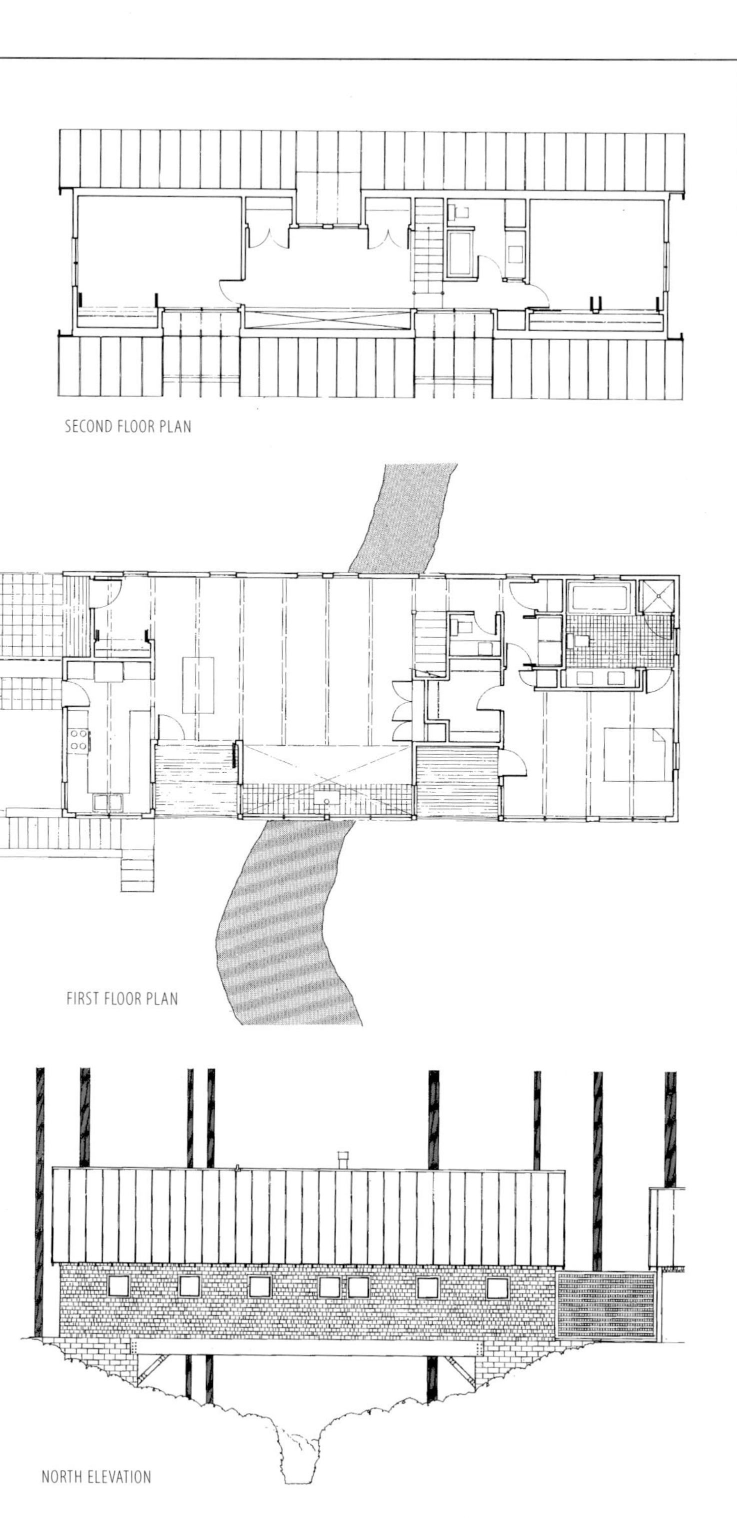

SECOND FLOOR PLAN

FIRST FLOOR PLAN

TRANSVERSAL SECTION

NORTH ELEVATION

The bridge over the wooded ravine enabled the house to have as little impact on the environment as possible. The building was tucked into the alder, cedar, and fir woods carefully, with only one tree felled during construction. Plywood and plasterboard are almost nonexistent in the house. Two covered balconies have galvanized railings.

The house is all wood construction except for the steel-reinforced, broken face concrete block abutment for the bridge. Fir-wrapped windows open up the view toward the waterfront. The kitchen cabinets are solid fir with a natural finish, and natural pine boards were used for the building's walls and floors. Glass blocks in the hearth of the wood stove give a view of the stream beneath the house.

Wall Buildings ▶

Larson Residence

BAINBRIDGE ISLAND, WASHINGTON

In a forest of madrona, cedar, and fir trees, the Larson Residence turns inward toward a formal courtyard to capture sunlight. Those trees—some of which are 120 feet (36 meters) tall—provide both a design constraint and the inspiration. This courtyard residence makes a "room" in the forest: this room is bounded by the interior spaces of the residence and "walls" of trees with openings to the forest.

The courtyard was conceived as a formal room, with highly ordered structure and openings. Providing a clear path for the sun over the treetops to the walls of the living area, a 30-foot x 50-foot (9-meter x 15-meter) courtyard gives a basic structure to the residence. This outdoor room includes surrounding walls, windows, and door openings, all commensurate with the scale of the yard.

The living spaces are shed elements that specifically respond to the owners' pattern of living and generally respond to the more random nature of the environment. In this dense tree canopy, the interior zones were placed around the court so that the most active (daytime) spaces get the most sunlight and the more passive (nighttime) rooms get the least. The whole of the residence is within a 100-foot- (30-meter-) diameter building lot, outside of which there is a permanent conservation zone.

LONGITUDINAL SECTION

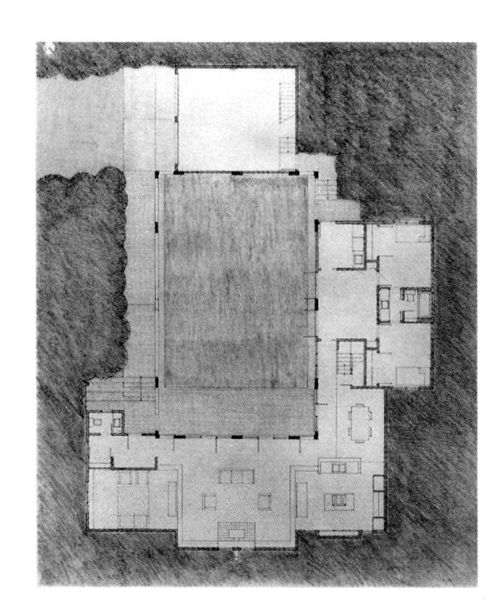

FIRST FLOOR PLAN

SECOND FLOOR PLAN

ROOF PLAN

NORTHWEST ELEVATION

On one side of the courtyard, openings mirror the windows in the walls of the house. In response to the woods, which are random and natural, a series of shed roofs is arrayed in an irregular pattern around the formal wall of the courtyard. The shed shapes are attached to the courtyard walls.

Strickland Residence

BAINBRIDGE ISLAND, WASHINGTON

This residence was conceived as two roof structures sitting atop two very long (130 foot/39 meter) parallel walls, in response to a very tight (28 foot/8 meter) lot with limited privacy on either side—yet with both a mountain view and water view. The client required a one-level, low-maintenance house with a garden and privacy in a crowded waterfront neighborhood.

The street side/entry roof covers a one-car garage and narrow entry passage that leads to an interior garden court. The second roof covers the 750-square-foot (67.5-square-meter) living area, with sleeping quarters connected to the kitchen by a ramp. The architect emphasized the 115-foot (34.5-meter) long load-bearing walls and gable roof in a linear design. The "walls" are punctuated by regular openings for their entire length, except at one corner that has views and privacy. Small, high windows at the upland side of the house maintain privacy, then lengthen into expansive vertical slots of glass at the waterfront side, as the walls curve down just enough to expose the southwest views.

The roof-bearing nature of the walls are further emphasized by their misalignment with the walls below the gables. By twisting these exterior surfaces out of parallel with the gable, the building receives the specific benefit of reinforcing one's comprehension of the structure.

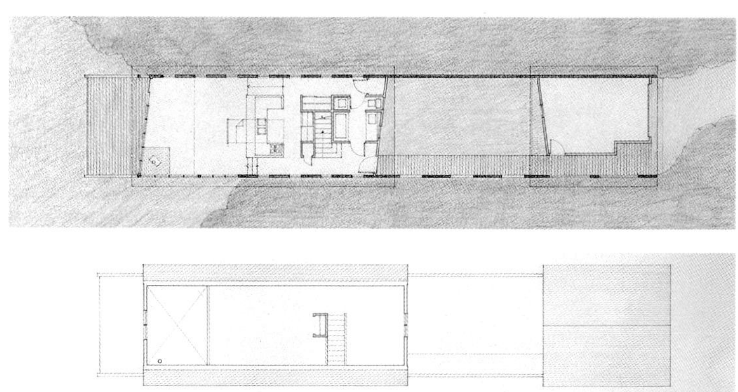

SITE PLAN (ABOVE), MAIN LEVEL (ABOVE RIGHT) AND LOFT LEVEL (BELOW RIGHT)

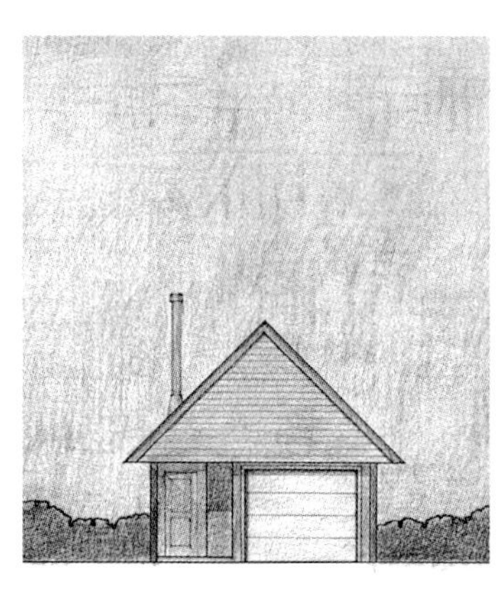

EAST ELEVATION

COURT ELEVATION

WEST ELEVATION

TRANSVERSAL SECTION

SOUTH ELEVATION

NORTH ELEVATION

Encompassing the view to the west, the waterfront side of the house is an expanse of glass. As part of the linear plan, the private garden is between the garage and house bound by side-walls with cutouts. To enable single-level living in a small space, the plan includes a pull-out trundle bed and a night stand.

Wright Guest House

THE HIGHLANDS, WASHINGTON

Part of an 8.5-acre (3.4-hectare) complex owned by art collectors, this guest residence fits into the landscape and is not visible from the main residence. To accomplish those two requests of the owners, the guest house is fitted into a natural depression in the surrounding forest. To further integrate this structure into the landscape it is dug into the depression as much as 14 feet (4 meters) below grade. It is accessed both by a "sculpture" trail from the main house and by a boardwalk through the forest.

By emphasizing the massive concrete wall, the architects attempted to reveal the weight of the earth and the weight of the materials used to retain it. The concrete was also used to visually contrast with the wooded "tent" that encloses the residence. Inside, the warm, gray-green concrete walls of the house serve as a foil for paintings and sculpture.

The wooden structure was twisted from the L-shaped concrete wall both to enlarge the entrance and constrict the elbow where the circulation passes from public to private zones. It was hoped that this misalignment of grids would also further heighten the contrast between the ephemeral wooden tent and the timeless concrete wall.

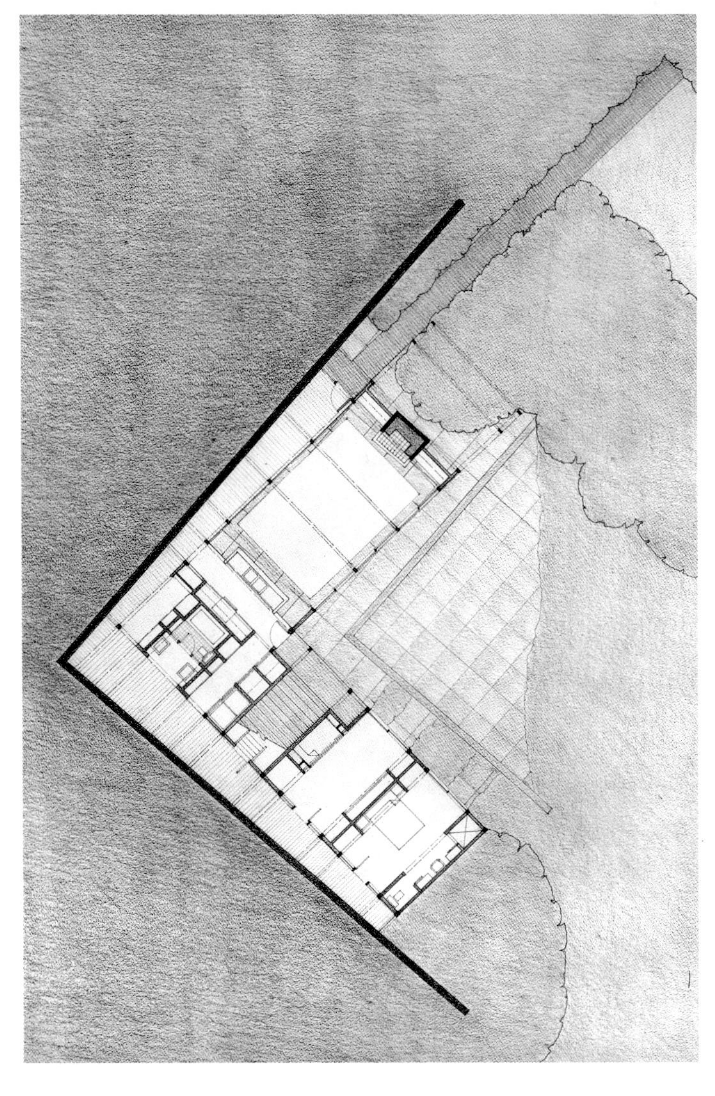

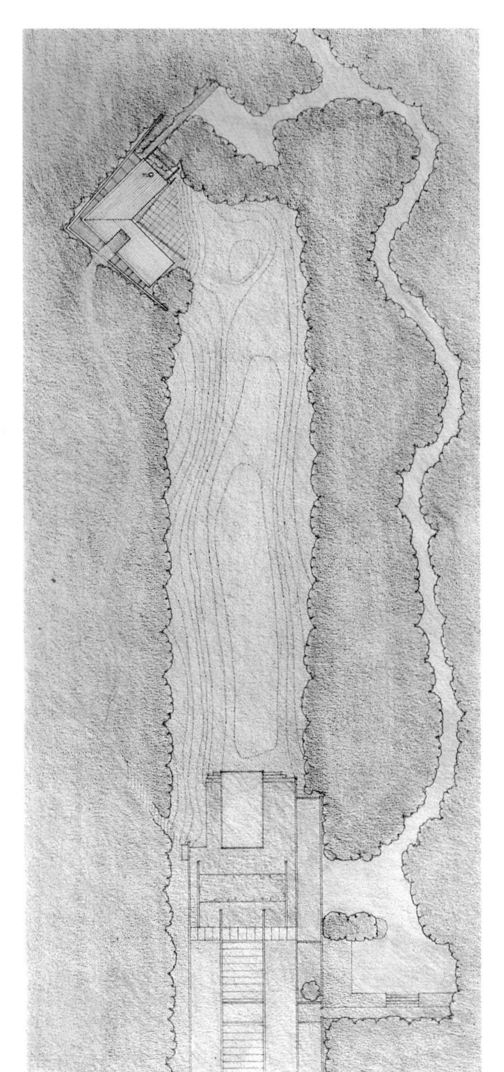

A secondary stairway rises within a protected alcove along the building's west elevation. Arcades composed of heavy timber "trees" define the north and south elevations. The stairway and bold wooden arcades take the place of grand interior lobbies, functioning as a transition between indoors and out.

Wright Guest House

The living-room hearth is twisted on the concrete floor. Broken concrete echoes the outside wall design. Fir woodwork contrasts with the gray concrete walls inside, echoing the balance of the transient present with a continuing past. The L-shaped guest house's outer concrete wall, fir framing, and cedar siding are fitted into the surrounding forest.

The approach to the house is through a skylit entry deck; the light from inside glows on the interior fir walls. Fiberglass ceiling panels extend the length of the hallways, serving as a gasket between the wooden building and the concrete wall. The wall and house are nonaligned, creating an entryway that tapers to a narrow passage. The wide end of the entry leads to the public spaces in the house, the narrow to the more private areas.

Guest House

MEDINA, WASHINGTON

Situated at the high end of a steep, suburban lot on Lake Washington, the 1,700-square-foot (153-square-meter) guest house was the first in a compound of buildings designed to combine state-of-the-art computer technology with environmental sensitivity. A joint venture with Peter Bohlin of Bohlin Cywinski Jackson, the complex includes a reception pavilion to seat 120, a boathouse, movie theater, trampoline room, swimming pool, and 20-car garage, in addition to the main residence.

The intent was to test managerial, aesthetic, and structural systems in this initial building before continuing with the rest of the complex. The guest house was sunken into the earth so that it would be barely visible from the entry drive. The residence is glass on two sides, where sliding panels open its interior to the outside; the remaining two walls are concrete.

One enters the house between two boardformed concrete walls, with light visible only in the distance, drawing the visitor into the earth-covered structure. Beyond an entry ramp lined with concrete columns, the building flattens and opens out to reveal the view and terrace. Inside, the concrete walls surrounding the hearth are broken away both to bring light into the space and to evoke a feeling of multiple occupations of the structure.

The earth-covered guest house—barely visible from the entry drive—draws visitors to the living/dining area through a dramatic entry featuring a row of concrete columns. The entries and interior provoke a study of light and space.

Guest House

Both the heavy timber framing and trim in the guest house are of recycled fir. The heavy steel bracing contrasts with the fir, which both complement the rough concrete and stone used throughout the building.

Sliding panels in the dining room open to the outside, and the floor paving continues from the inside space to the outside. Massive 4-inch x 12-inch (10 cm x 30.5 cm) beams span 14 feet (4 meters). All came from old-growth timbers recycled from an old industrial building, disassembled, and re-milled locally.

Guest House

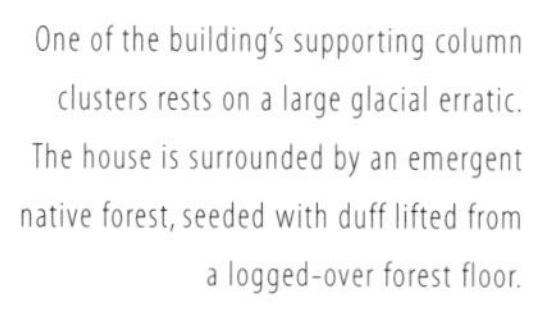

One of the building's supporting column clusters rests on a large glacial erratic. The house is surrounded by an emergent native forest, seeded with duff lifted from a logged-over forest floor.

Garage

MEDINA, WASHINGTON

To accommodate the owner's need for a large garage that would not dominate the land, this vaulted structure is dug deep enough into the earth to be invisible from the drive above. The steep hillside prohibited road construction, so drivers approach the 10,000-square-foot garage by driving in front of it on a heavy wooden trestle. The trestle is supported by branching clusters of columns that resemble big-leafed maple trees that cover the adjacent hillsides. The garage extends back into the hillside to a depth of 75 feet (22.5 meters) below grade level. Knowing that this deep an excavation would cut through several aquifers, the architects channeled the flow into a 100,000 gallon (380,000 liter) cistern that is formed by the 5-foot (1.5 meter) deep arch restraining grade beams. The water will be used for irrigation and wetland maintenance on other areas of the land.

Between the concrete arches, the vaulted roof is broken away into an interstitial space that reveals octagonal columns holding a second lid. That roof is tilted at the angle of the hillside. The pure arched forms are therefore juxtaposed with the random demands of the earth. Skylights allow light to penetrate from the rear of the building. The project is a joint venture with Peter Bohlin of Bohlin Cywinski Jackson.

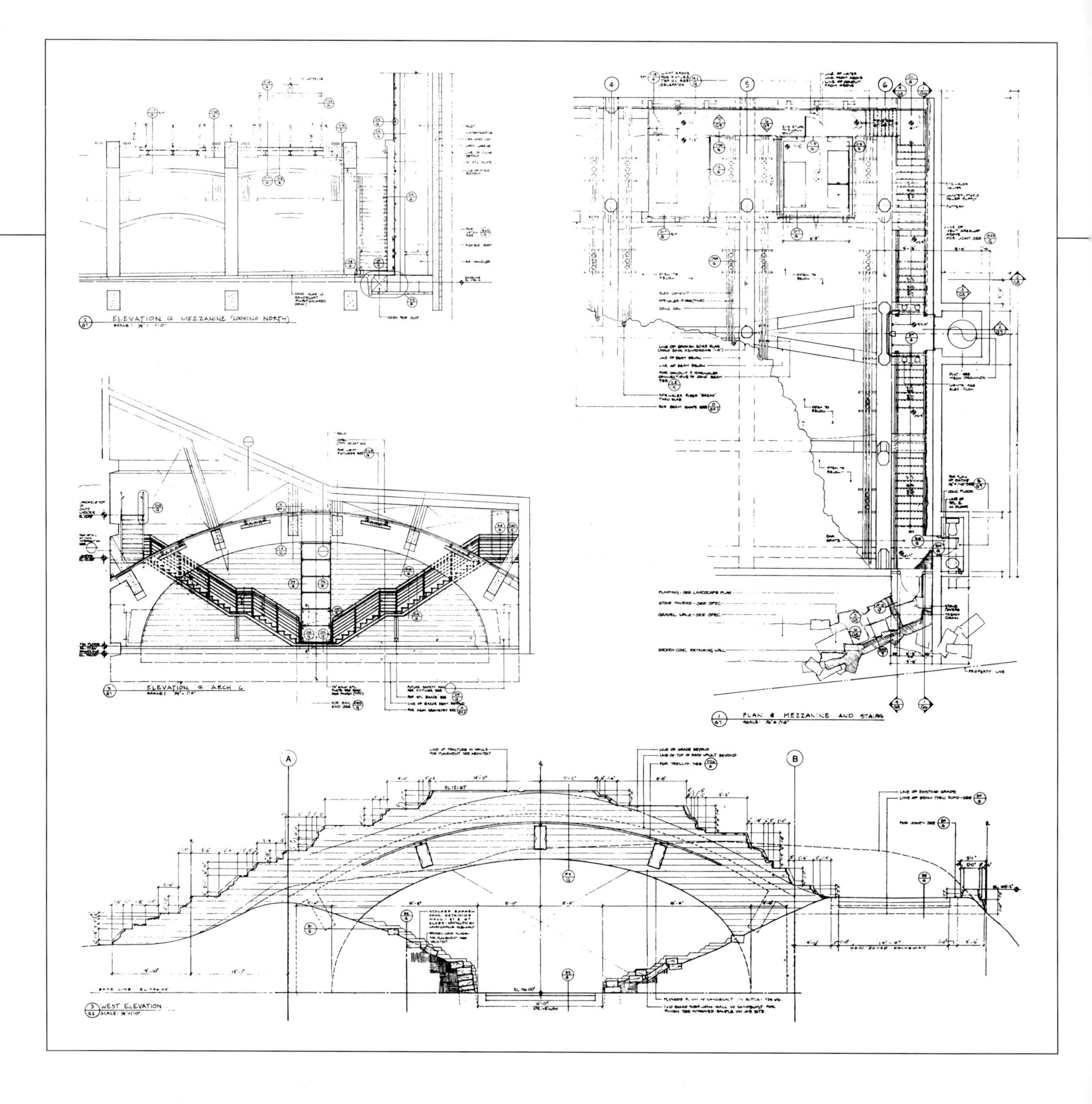

ELEVATION @ MEZZANINE (LOOKING NORTH)
ELEVATION @ ARCH 6
PLAN @ MEZZANINE AND STAIRS
OPEN TO BELOW
PLANTING - SEE LANDSCAPE PLAN
STONE PAVERS - SEE SPEC.
GRAVEL WALK - SEE SPEC.
BROKEN CONC. RETAINING WALL
PROPERTY LINE
WEST ELEVATION
NEW PAVED DRIVEWAY
DRIVEWAY

The garage holds twenty vehicles or two hundred sixty people. The arches are high enough, and the space large enough, for a women's collegiate basketball court. A key will eventually be etched into the concrete. The face of the garage is visible from the drive; skylights are the only sign from above that there is any structure there at all.

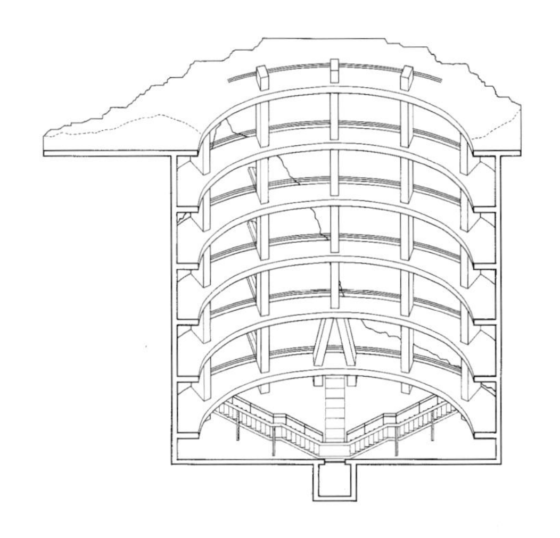

Steel braces and stairway contrast with the boardformed concrete, colored to appear weathered and warm. The octagonal columns above the arches are lit at night to reveal the true nature of the structure and the uniqueness of the earth above. Speakers are hidden in the walls of the garage, meeting the owner's requirement that technology be incorporated into the building.

Swimming Pool

MEDINA, WASHINGTON

Designed as a joint venture with Peter Bohlin of Bohlin Cywinski Jackson Architects and part of a large residential complex on the east side of Lake Washington near Seattle, this swimming pool building is covered with earth and set into a hillside. Like other buildings in the complex, it accommodates a need for integration of computer technology with environmental sensitivity. The 20-foot x 60-foot (6-meter x 18-meter) lap pool is in a heavy timber building. All of the structure is fabricated from timbers recycled from dismantled industrial buildings. High-definition video displays are hidden by wooden panels that fit into the slatted-wood walls.

Meticulous attention was paid to details in the pool building, evident in the wood diving board, tile stairs, and stone handholds. Other features demonstrate the mix of nature and technology: glass walls open automatically to the outside; fiberglass skylights allow diffused light into the lower areas of the building; and clerestories bring in light to the higher pool space. A shower behind the large granite slab acts as the entrance to the sauna.

(Top) The timber in the building came from a sawmill that was scheduled for demolition. The swimming pool complex is made of stone and wood. (Overleaf) A smaller pool connects both the inside of the building and the outer yard, passing beneath glass panels.

Swimming Pool

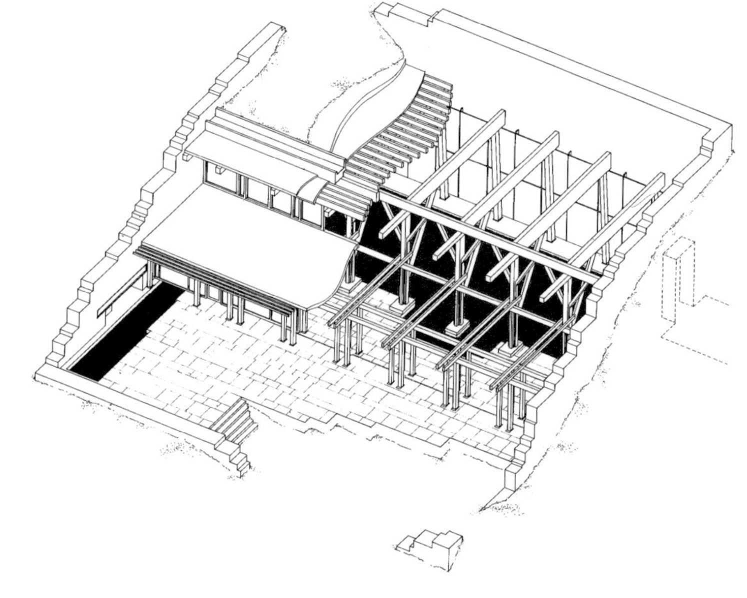

Fiberglass skylights light the building from above, since it is dug into the earth. Glass panels in the front of the building open automatically on warm days. The pool building includes details such as the wood diving board, tile stairs, and stone handholds.

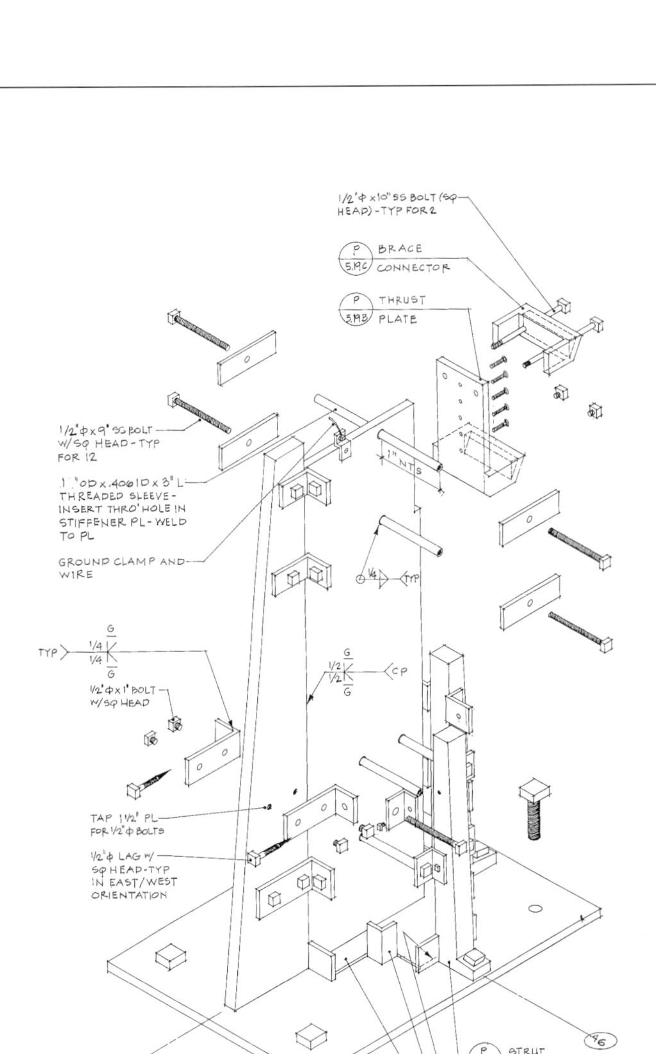

Wood, stone, tile, and steel form the palette of materials for the pool building. Soaring ceilings are anchored with huge beams and highly-detailed steel connectors to the stone floor. Hidden sliding panels reveal high-resolution video screens.

Frame Buildings ▶

Virginia Merrill Bloedel Education Center

BAINBRIDGE ISLAND, WASHINGTON

Located on the 150-acre (60-hectare) Bloedel Reserve on Bainbridge Island, Washington, a building that will ultimately be a lecture hall began life as a memorial to the owner's 62 years of marriage. The 89-year-old client, owner of a semi-public estate of gardens, asked for a building with a view of his wife's unmarked grave, located at the end of an existing reflecting pool.

The stone supports of the future Education Center were set on an axis with the gravesite. Exposed heavy timber posts and beams carry the structural load. Stone plinths support the superstructure, which spans across an intermittent water course. The entry walk centers the axis through the building to a viewing deck. The line of the axis continues through woods into an open meadow where it is marked by a boulder before it goes on to reach the gravesite.

The owner's bedroom is twisted so that his bed is also aligned on-axis with the grave site. The stone and wooden structure of the 1,400-square-foot (126-square-meter) building is carefully fitted into its forest context. The organic wooden structure will someday decay, but the stone elements will always be there as a symbol of the owner's relationship with his wife.

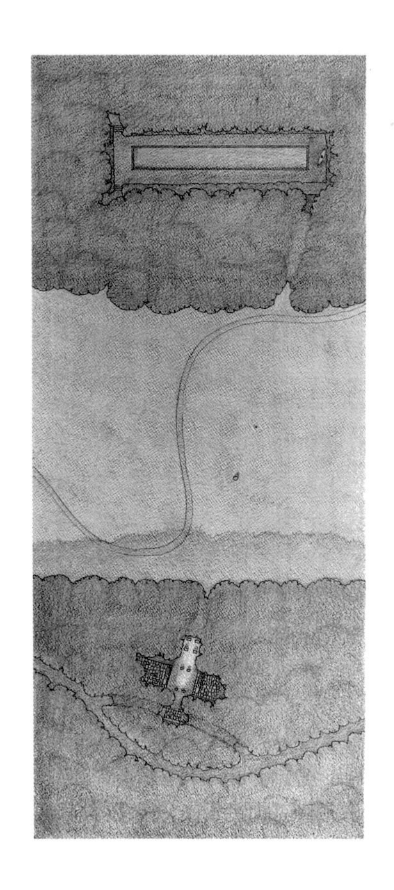
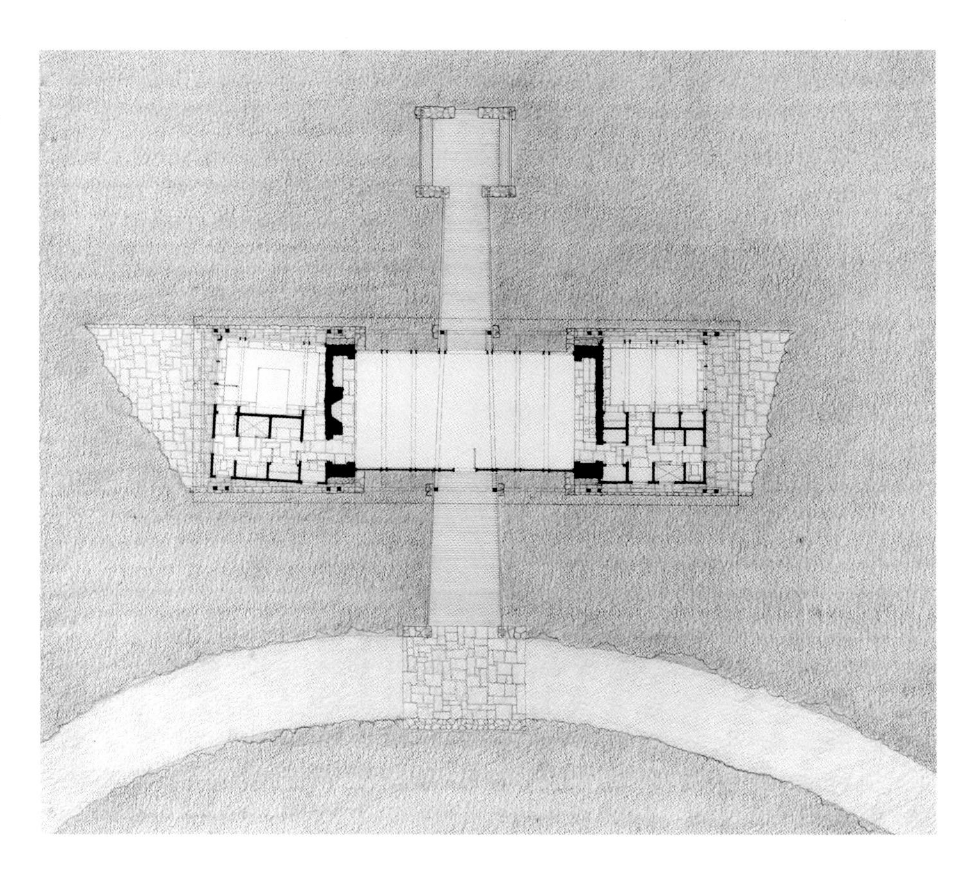

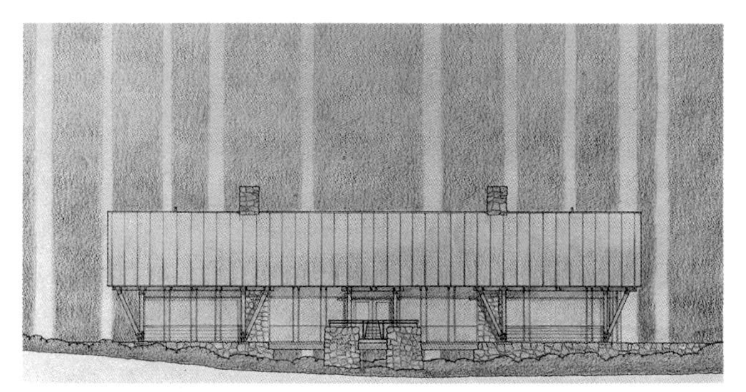

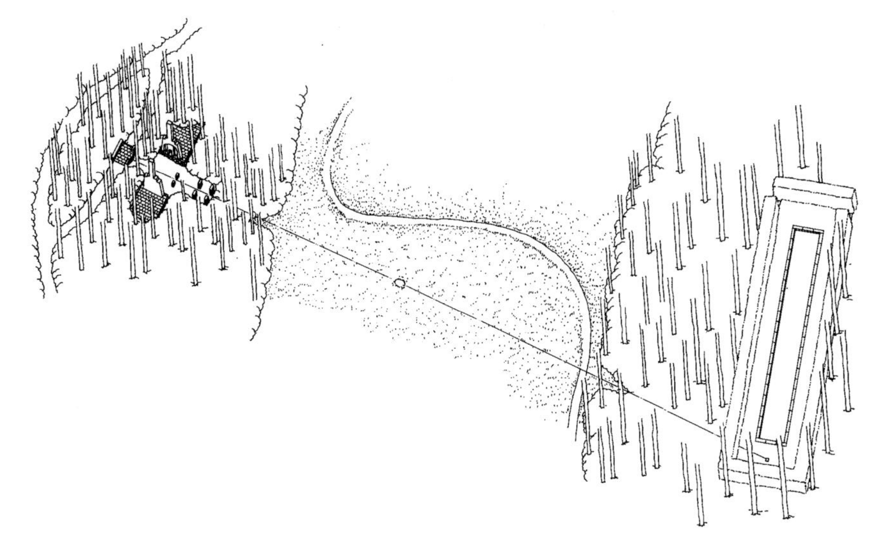

(Overleaf) The beams at the central doorway are doubled, symbolizing the couple's long partnership. The wooden deck, supported by large stone piers, carries the axis toward the gravesite.

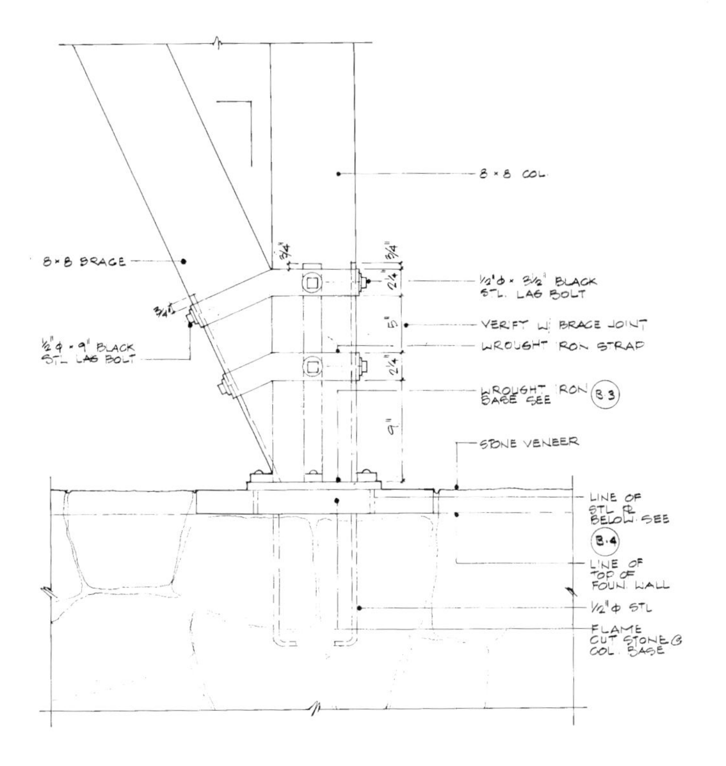

Exposed heavy timber posts and beams carry the structural load. Stone plinths support the superstructure, which spans across an intermittent water course, continuing through the woods into an open meadow. The plinths are on axis with the unmarked grave.

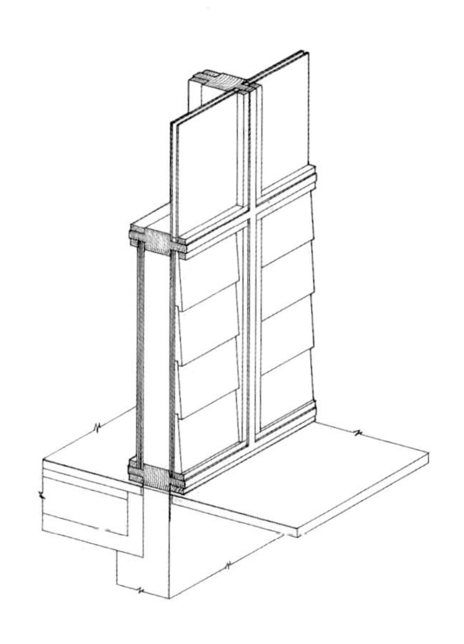

Inside the building, paired stone arches reinforce the symmetry of the gravesite axis. At opposite ends of the room, stone walls with inset doorways echo the stone piers that support the building.

Two bedroom suites at each end of the building will eventually be guest rooms for visiting lecturers. The furniture was also designed by the architect to fit with the revealed wood structure.

Paulk Residence

SEABECK, WASHINGTON

Perched on a 200-foot (60-meter) waterfront bluff, the Paulk residence commands a strong view of the Olympic Mountains despite being nestled in a dense forest. Fitted into the forest on the remnants of an old logging road, the house is anchored to the ground at its south end, then floats 15 feet (4.5 meters) high as the ground falls away beneath it at the north end. The design attempts to reveal the nature of place, the materials, and their role in making the shelter.

Faced with a required 80-foot (24-meter) setback from the edge of an upward-sloping bluff, the view was accommodated by allowing the building to rise out of grade as it moved east. A 130-foot (39-meter) entry ramp passes through the building, emerging from the opposite side to lead to a belvedere high over the cliff. Since the forest was relatively undisturbed by construction (only three trees were felled), the bridge offers an opportunity for guests to intimately experience the forest as they move through it.

On the inside, the ceiling is pulled back in places, revealing the nature of the construction materials. Framing in the foyer is exposed; floor joists are cut at random lengths. In places, sheet metal is screwed into place as soffits or wall panels.

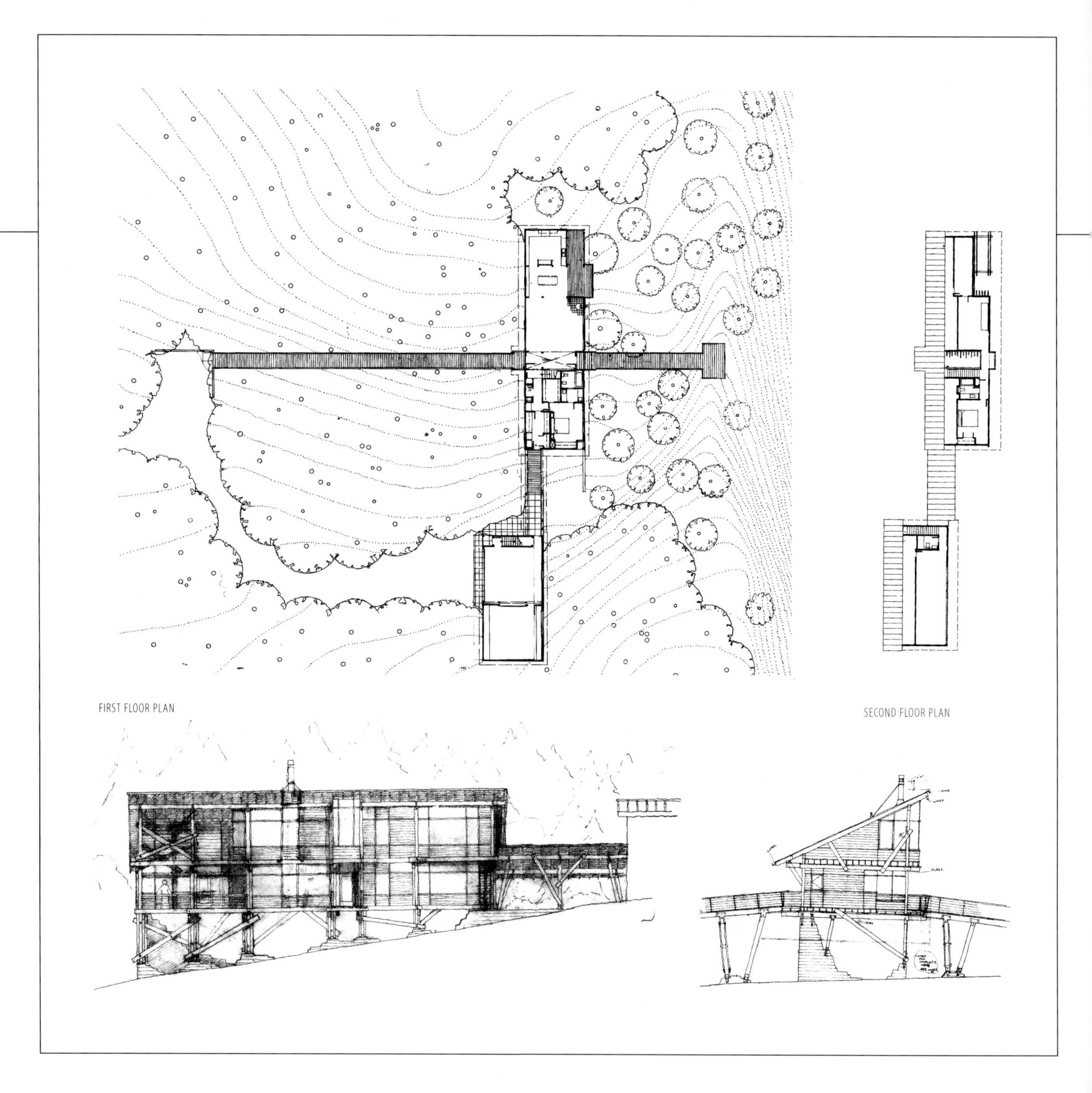
FIRST FLOOR PLAN
SECOND FLOOR PLAN

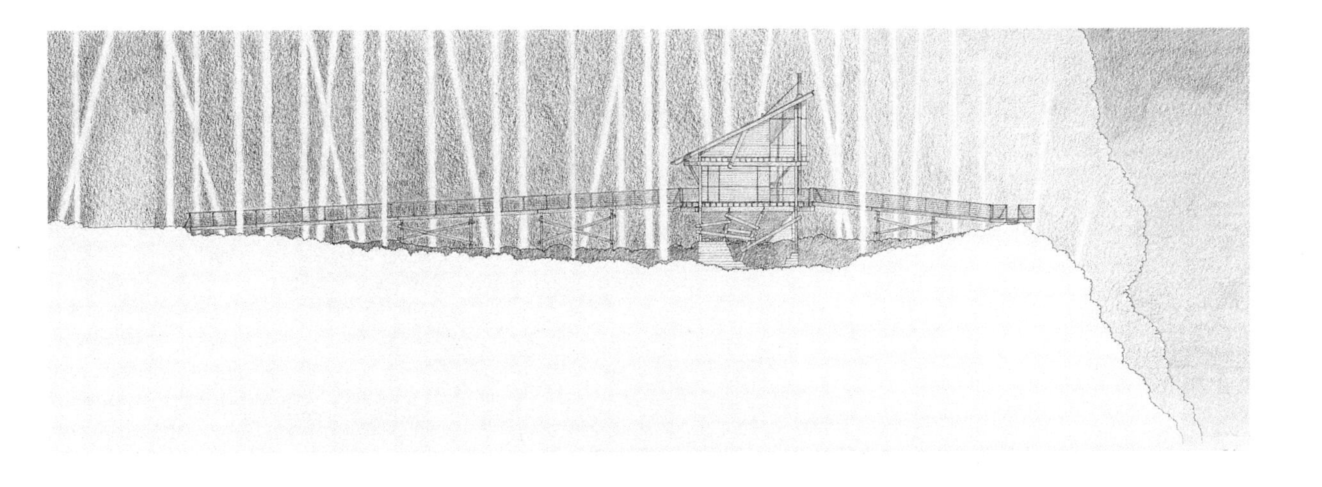

The long wooden ramp leading to the entrance accommodates a site of perverse contours. The bridge is supported by wood posts on concrete plinths, and the entry door is surrounded by glass.

Construction was designed to create minimal disturbance of the forest. At one point, the roof and rafters were notched to preserve a tree. The haphazard, cross-braced posts under the house are expressive of the ad hoc nature of the support.

Paulk Residence

The view of trees and water is seen from inside through a 22-foot (7-meter) tall grid of glass. Each of the nine rooms, except for the laundry, has a view.

Giving clues to the nature of the materials used in construction, the ceiling is pulled back in places to reveal the rafters. Framing in the foyer is exposed; floor joists are cut at random lengths; and sheet metal is screwed into place as soffits or wall panels. Maple floors and pine paneling are treated with a transparent white stain.

Houdek/Pope Residence

SEABECK, WASHINGTON

The owners wanted to build a 3,000-square-foot (270-square-meter) home without destroying the site's huge fir, cedar, and maple trees, but realized that the narrow site was limited by the ravine and its resident stream. In response to the circumstance of this heavily forested waterfront ravine, the architects elected to design a building on a trestle that spans 140 feet (42 meters) at an elevation 18 feet (5 meters) above the ravine's bottom. By designing this kind of structure, the land—and its living systems—were disturbed as little as possible. The footings were hand-excavated and the trestle structure acted as a staging platform for the construction of a series of simple "boxes" that sit on and over the trestle.

This series of wooden buildings resting atop the trestle provides outdoor space between the garage, living area, bedrooms, and kitchen. The use of natural light is integral to the design: in the kitchen, for example, translucent fiberglass skylights allow soft, diffused light into the building. The trestle itself is given as much expression as the individual buildings as it moves through the trees, resulting in a residence that resembles a long bridge with a row of houses on it—all traversing the site among the treetops.

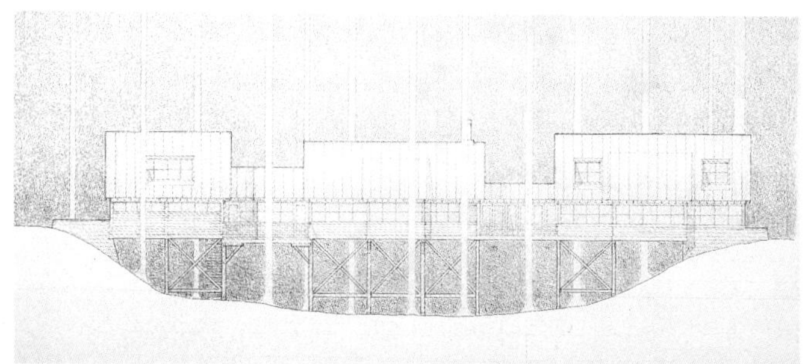

The trestle supports imitate a key feature of the site. A cedar tree grows below the house from a decaying, 6-foot- (2-meter-) diameter "nurse log." Eventually, the log will dissolve, leaving the cedar raised up on its roots, somewhat like the house is, set upon the trestle.

The wooden trestle raises the residence 18–19 feet off the ground so that living spaces are in the treetops. The house is constructed of all wood, with some plasterboard. Translucent fiberglass skylights over the kitchen allow soft, diffused light to enter the building.

Waterman Cabin

SNAKE RIVER, IDAHO

Taking its inspiration from ancient mining residue found on site, this wilderness fishing cabin resembles a miner's shack. The building was constructed with light materials, dictated by the remote building site 35 miles (56 kilometers) upriver from Lewiston, Idaho—all of the construction materials were shipped to the site via barges—and by the fact that the owner wanted to build the 400-square-foot (36-square-meter) cabin himself with the help of his sons.

The firm's first desert project forced the architects to conceive of a building that would "fit," but without the benefit of an enclosing forest. A survey of the site revealed a bowl-shaped dip in the earth where there was once mining activity. After carefully surveying the land, they chose that small undulation in the contour of the steep hillside to "tuck" the building in. Then they chose to design a structure that would make the building not only light in construction but to appear that way as well.

Multi-paned windows yield views of the Snake River, which the building faces. The intention was to make the cabin appear transitional, not disturbing the landscape. The shape was derived from a combination of the proper sun angles for its roof-mounted photovoltaic power generation, and from old desert "shacks" that can still be seen along some areas of the river.

Waterman Cabin

All the materials had to be barged to the cabin site. The building was lightly framed, with braces visibly supporting the structure. The cabin has only two rooms, plus a small bathroom with a composting toilet. Clerestories allow light to enter on the east side. Multi-paned windows look out onto the river.

Gunnelson Cabin

BALLARD LAKE, WISCONSIN

This 500-square-foot (45-square-meter) fishing cabin was fitted into the landscape with a minimum of disturbance. The 8-foot- (2-meter-) thick "core" element houses a kitchen, bath, sleeping loft and basement mechanical room. The 20-foot (6-meter) living room/bedroom/deck is cantilevered out over the surrounding landscape. The "tipped tree" columns are designed to fit in with the forest when one is inside the building.

Built by the owner and a friend, the cabin is anchored at one end with a stone base. The solid core provides space for the mechanical functions: basement, furnace, and bathroom, with a sleeping loft above. The remainder of the cabin and the deck float 8 feet (2 meters) off the forest floor. The walls of the one-room living area comprise high-performance glass, most of the way down to the floor. Beds are built into the walls in the area below the glass.

The living space was created in response to the extreme seasonal changes in the climate—the glass walls promote warmth in winter months; but in the summer the windows swing up to the ceiling and the deck doors fold back to create a large screened porch. This hovering room not only connects the owners to their land visually, but connects them acoustically as well.

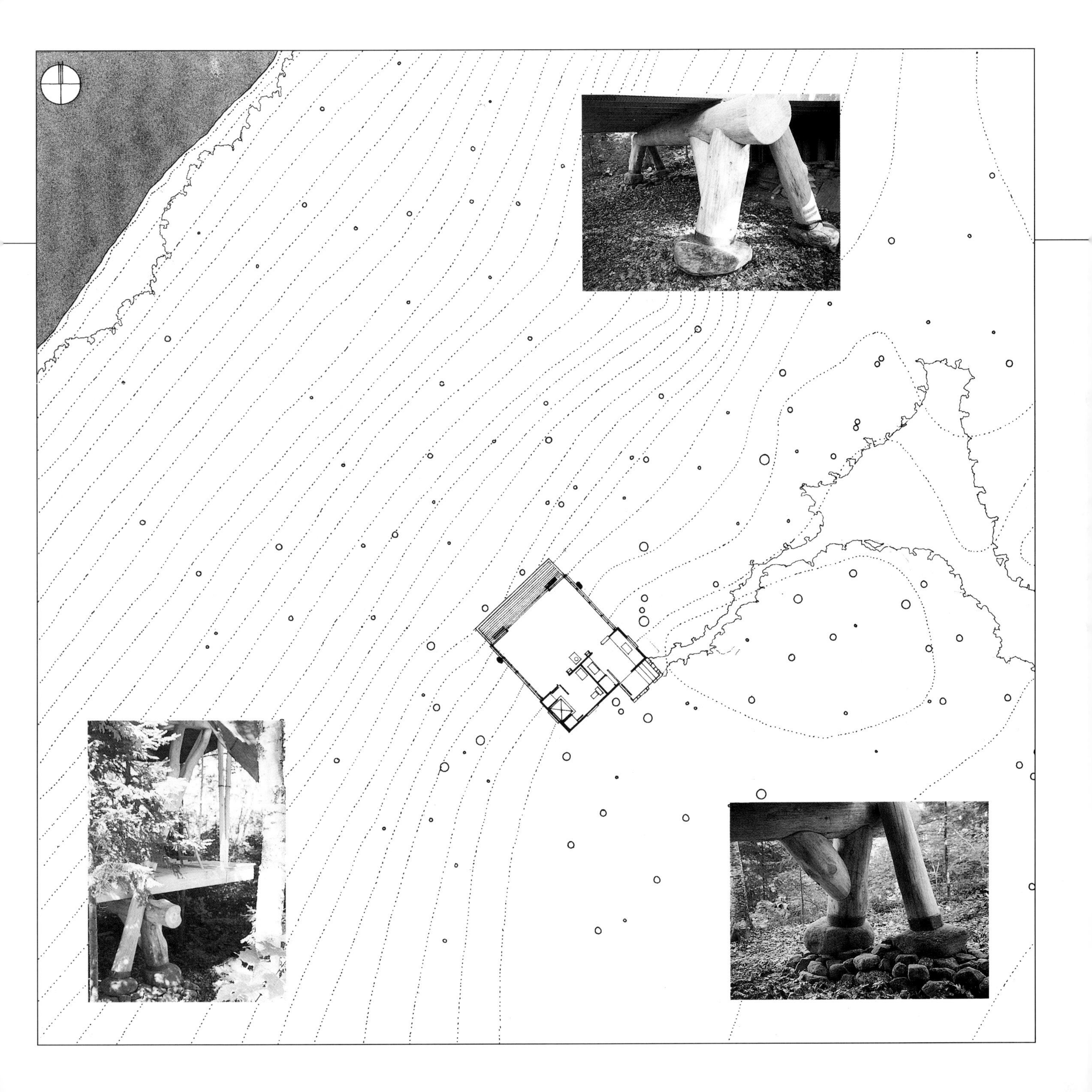

JOHN WILLARD
HANGED
AUGUST 19, 1692

Memorials ▶

Salem Witch Trials Tercentenary Memorial

SALEM, MASSACHUSETTS

In an attempt to give form to concepts of injustice, the Salem Witch Trials Tercentenary Memorial is the result of a collaboration between artist and architect. The architect worked with artist Maggie Smith, winning an international competition for the design of the memorial in 1991. The intent of the memorial was to commemorate the trials and execution of twenty innocent people suspected of witchcraft in 1692. Situated on a 5,000-square-foot (450-square-meter) plot surrounded by a seventeenth-century cemetery—in which many of the citizens of the 1692 community are buried—the memorial features a wall in which earth was dug out, making visitors feel as if they are standing in an actual grave.

The designers defined "injustice" with four words: Silence, Deafness, Persecution, and Memory. To represent Silence, they graded and organized the site to emphasize the surrounding tombstones as silent watchers, mutely looking into the memorial. For Deafness they inscribed the historical protests of innocence on the entry threshold and had them slide under the stone wall in mid-sentence. For Persecution they planted black locust trees, from which these innocents were believed to be hanged. For Memory, the names, dates, and manners of death of the executed were inscribed on stone slabs and then cantilevered as benches from the stone wall.

I DO PLEAD
DENY IT TO MY DYING

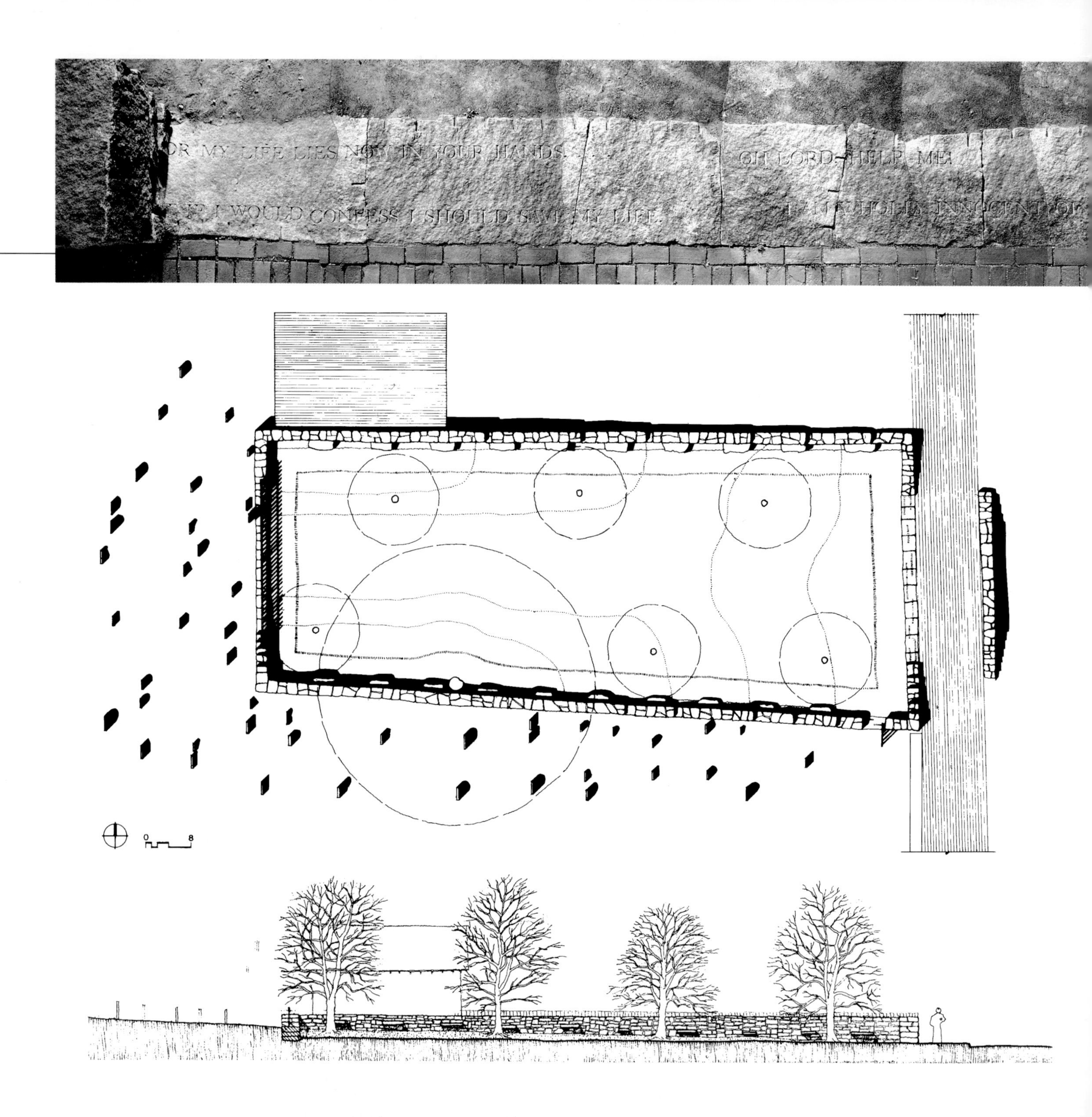
OR MY LIFE LIES NOW IN YOUR HANDS.
IF I WOULD CONFESS I SHOULD SAVE MY LIFE.
OH LORD HELP ME!
I AM WHOLLY INNOCENT OF
0
8

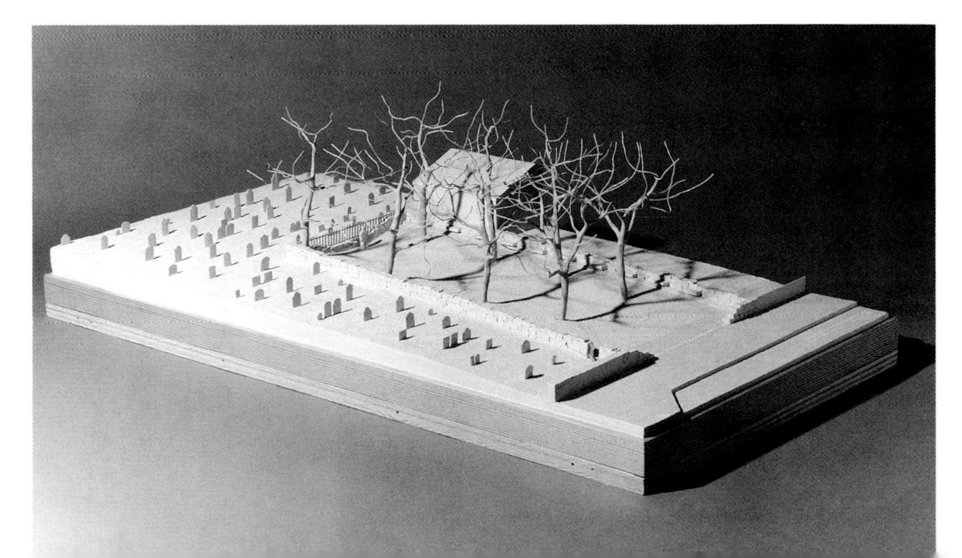

Protestations of innocence mark the threshold to the memorial. The victims' words, which run under the stone wall in mid-sentence—symbolizing the crushed truth—were taken from court records. Tombstones in the adjacent cemetery mark the resting places of the victims' neighbors. A barred iron fence and rough granite walls divide the cemetery from the memorial, emphasizing the confrontation of persecutor and victim.

Salem Witch Trials Tercentenary Memorial

The wall of the memorial was made out of weathered granite, taken from an abandoned New Hampshire quarry. The pieces were put in place with crowbars and wedges, much like the farm fences of years past. The twenty stone benches around the perimeter are inscribed with the victims' names and execution dates. These are the first markers for the victims in three hundred years. A seventeenth-century typeface was used for the inscriptions.

Armed Forces Memorial

NORFOLK, VIRGINIA

A second collaboration with artist Maggie Smith resulted in the winning of a design competition to produce an Armed Forces Memorial in Norfolk, Virginia. The design was inspired by a quote from Abraham Lincoln about the sacrifices of the individual in war. That quote is displayed prominently at the departure point of the memorial.

In order to create a separate place of contemplation, the designers bounded an existing point in Norfolk Harbor with a fortification-like brick enclosure. This enclosure is then accessed from the existing waterfront park via two bridges. Next, the designers conceived of an enclosed plaza strewn with wind-blown letters.

The letters, three times life-size and cast in bronze, are scattered on the plaza as if they were thrown into the wind. Each bronze plate features a quote from a letter written by someone serving in war, written within a month of his or her death. Some of the letters are love letters; others describe the anguish that war brings. Taken together, they were chosen and edited to reveal the full range of thoughts, beliefs, and emotions of Americans serving in armed conflicts from 1775–1992.

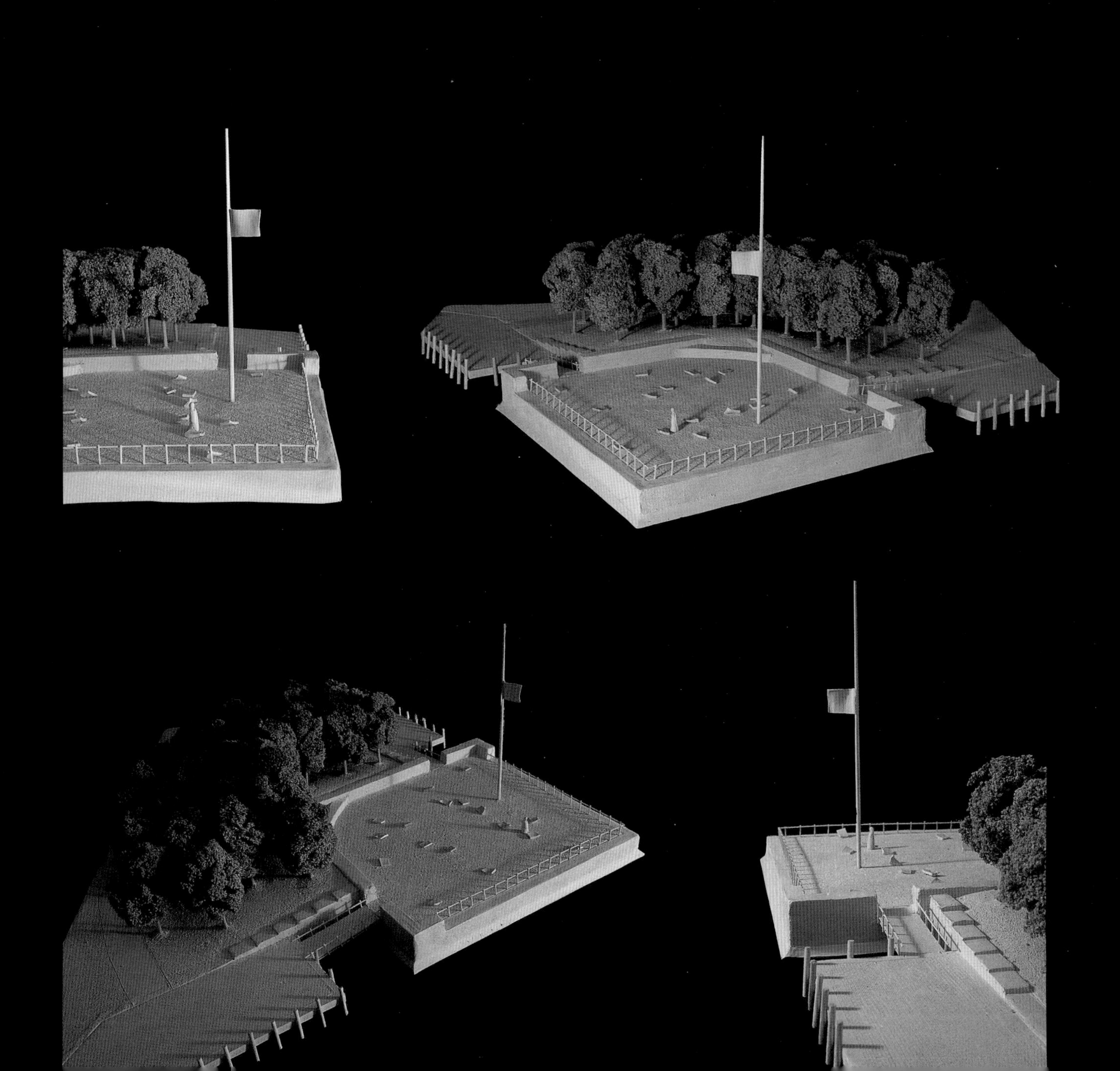

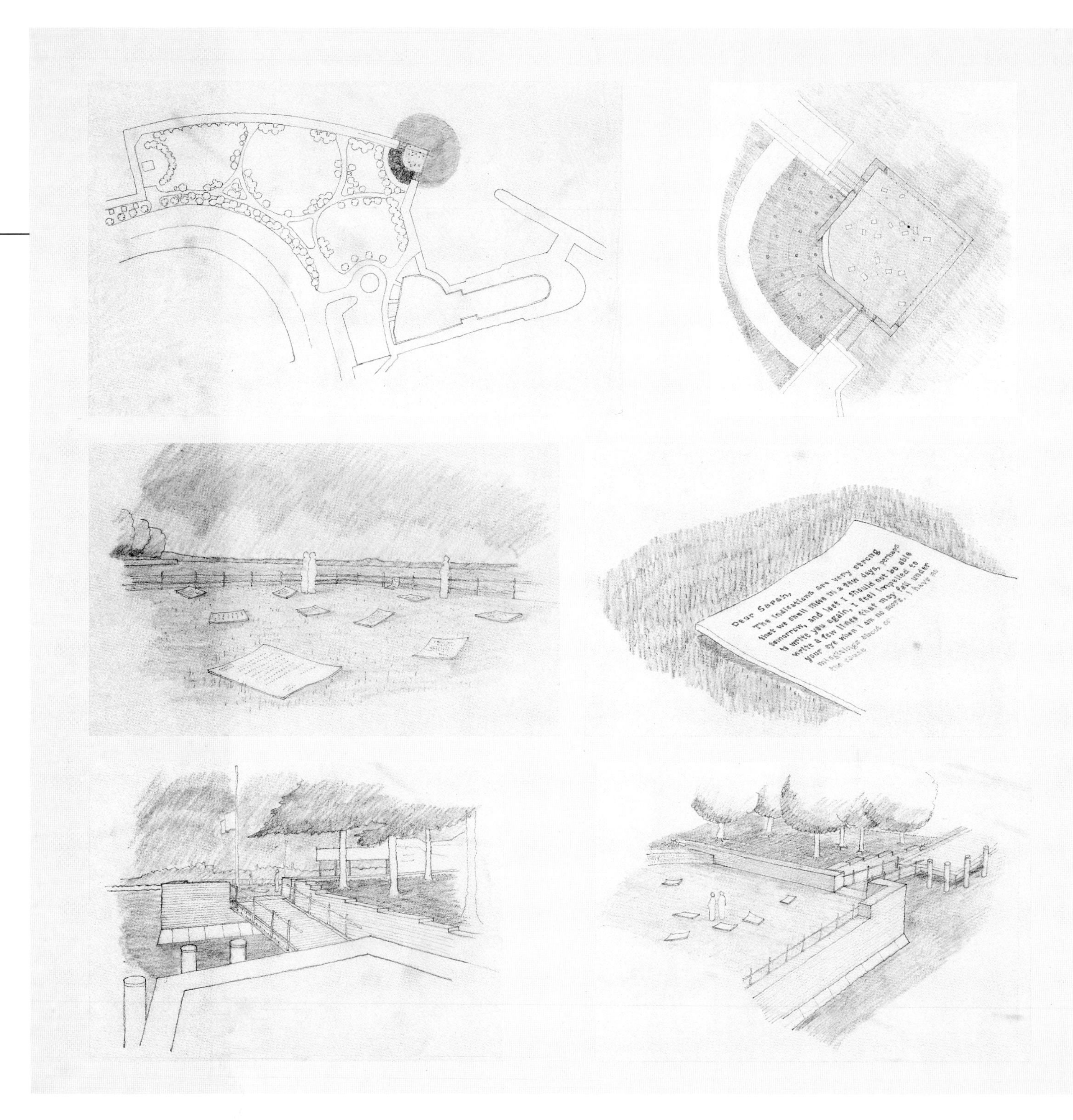
Dear Sarah,
The indications are very strong
that we shall move in a few days, perhaps
tomorrow, and lest I should not be able
to write you again, I feel impelled to
write a few lines that may fall under
your eye when I am no more.

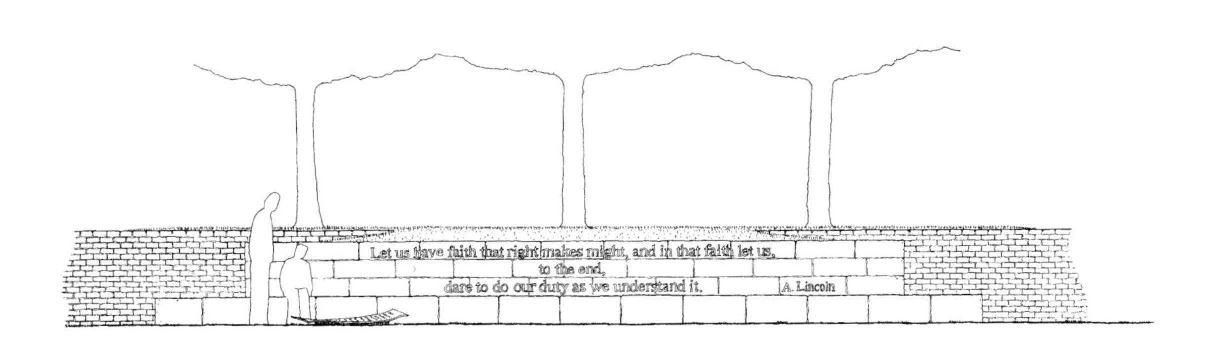

The letters for the projects were mocked up at one-third scale and hand-molded to capture the feeling of the wind blowing them in from across the ocean.

July 14, 1861
My Very Dear Wife,
The indications are very strong that we
shall move in a few days, perhaps tomorrow,
and lest I should not be able to write you
again I feel impelled to write a few lines
that may fall under your eye when I am no
more.... I have no misgivings about or lack
of confidence in the cause in which I am
engaged, and my courage does not halt or
falter....Sarah, my love for you is deathless.
It seems to bind me with mighty cables that
nothing but Omnipotence can break and yet
my love of country comes over me like a
strong wind and bears me irresistibly with
all those chains to the battlefield. The
memories of all the blissful moments I
have enjoyed with you come crowding over
me, and I feel most deeply grateful to God
and you that I have enjoyed them so
long....If I do not [return], my dear Sarah,
never forget how much I loved you....
Sullivan Ballou
d. July 21, 1861

Appendix ▶

List of Works and Credits

DAUBENBERGER RESIDENCE; Port Townsend, Washington, 1979
Awards: AIA Seattle Honor Award 1981
AIA/Western Red Cedar Association Merit Award 1981
AIA/Sunset/Western Homes Award Citation 1983
Client: Donna and Jim Daubenberger
Project Team: Jim Cutler, FAIA
Contractor: Owner
Photographer: Vern Green

PARKER RESIDENCE; Bainbridge Island, Washington, 1984
Awards: AIA National Honor Award 1986
AIA Seattle Honor Award 1985
AIA/Western Red Cedar Association First Award 1985
AIA/Sunset/Western Homes Award Merit Award 1984
Client: Jim and Lucille Parker
Project Team: Jim Cutler, FAIA, Amy Hiatt
Contractor: Colegrove Brothers Construction
Photographer: Art Grice

CATSKILLS RESIDENCE; Lew Beach, New York, 1990
Client: Bing and Migs Wright
Project Team: Jim Cutler, FAIA, Bruce Anderson, AIA
Contractor: Noel Graybill Construction
Photographers: Peter Aaron/Esto (p. 25 middle, bottom), Jim Cutler (p. 22, 23, 25 top)

THE BRIDGE HOUSE; Bainbridge Island, Washington, 1987
Awards: AIA/Wood Council Merit Award 1989
AIA/Western Red Cedar Association Merit Award 1989
AIA/Sunset/Western Homes Award Citation 1991
Seattle Times/AIA Home of the Year Honor Award 1988
Client: Gale Cool
Project Team: Jim Cutler, FAIA, Jeff Garlid
Contractor: James McDonald Kennedy
Structural Engineer: Greg Hiatt
Photographers: Peter Aaron/Esto (p. 27, 30 middle, 31), Art Grice (p. 26, 29, 30 bottom), Jim Cutler (p. 30 top)

LARSON RESIDENCE; Bainbridge Island, Washington, 1981
Awards: AIA Seattle Merit Award 1983
AIA/Sunset/Western Homes Award Citation 1984
Client: Patsy and Steve Larson
Project Team: Jim Cutler, FAIA, Bruce Anderson, AIA, Amy Hiatt
Contractor: Ron Brown Construction
Photographers: Vern Green (p. 34, 35, 37 top), Art Grice (37 middle, bottom)

STRICKLAND RESIDENCE; Bainbridge Island, Washington, 1986
Awards: AIA/Western Red Cedar Association Merit Award 1987
AIA/Sunset/Western Homes Awards Merit Award 1987
Client: Norma Strickland
Project Team: Jim Cutler, FAIA, Bruce Anderson, AIA
Contractor: Monte Hall Construction
Photographers: Art Grice, James Cutler Architects (p. 40 middle, left)

WRIGHT GUEST HOUSE; The Highlands, Washington, 1987
Awards: AIA Seattle Honor Award 1988
AIA/Wood Council Merit Award 1988
Client: Bagely and Virgina Wright
Project Team: Jim Cutler, FAIA, Bruce Anderson, AIA, Amy Hiatt
Contractor: Charter Construction, Inc.
Structural Engineer: Greg Hiatt
Photographers: Peter Aaron/Esto (p. 42, 43, 45 top, 48, 49, 50, 51 top), Art Grice (p. 45 middle, bottom, 51 middle, bottom), Langdon Clay (p. 46, 47)

GUEST HOUSE; Medina, Washington, 1993
(joint venture with Bohlin Cywinski Jackson)
Client: Private
Project Team: from JCA: Jim Cutler, FAIA, Pat Munter, Bruce Anderson, AIA; from BCJ: Peter Bohlin, FAIA, Theresa Thomas, Russ Hamlet, Robert Miller
Contractor: Sellen Construction Co., Inc.
Landscape Architect: The Berger Partnership
Structural Engineer: KPFF Consulting Engineers
Mechanical/Electrical Engineer: Interface Engineering, Inc.
Photographers: Karl Backus (p. 53, 55 middle, 56 bottom, 58, 59, 62 top and bottom, 63), Art Grice (p. 52, 55 top, bottom, 56 top, middle, 57, 60, 61, 62 middle)

GARAGE; Medina, Washington, 1992
(joint venture with Bohlin Cywinski Jackson)
Client: Private
Project Team: from JCA: Jim Cutler, FAIA, Pat Munter, Bruce Anderson, AIA, Dave Cinamon, Lydia Marshall, Nick Reid; from BCJ: Peter Bohlin, FAIA, Terrence Wagner, Robert Miller, Don Maxwell
Contractor: Sellen Construction Co., Inc.
Landscape Architect: The Berger Partnership
Structural Engineer: KPFF Consulting Engineers
Mechanical/Electrical Engineer: Interface Engineering, Inc.
Photographers: Chris Eden (p. 65, 67 bottom, 68, 69), Art Grice (p. 67 top), Pat Munter (p. 64 left)

SWIMMING POOL; Medina, Washington, 1995
(joint venture with Bohlin Cywinski Jackson)
Client: Private
Project Team: from JCA: Jim Cutler, FAIA, Pat Munter, Bruce Anderson, AIA, Stephen Rising; from BCJ: Peter Bohlin, FAIA, Bill Loose, Shane Chandler
Contractor: Sellen Construction Co., Inc.
Landscape Architect: The Berger Partnership
Structural Engineer: KPFF Consulting Engineers
Mechanical/Electrical Engineer: Interface Engineering, Inc.
Photographers: Art Grice, Lydia Marshall (p. 73 top)

VIRGINIA MERRILL BLOEDEL EDUCATION CENTER; Bloedel Reserve, Bainbridge Island, Washington, 1992
Awards: AIA National Honor Award 1993
AIA Northwest Regional AIA 1994
AIA Seattle Honor Award 1992
AIA/Wood Council Honor Award 1992
Client: Prentice Bloedel
Project Team: Jim Cutler, FAIA, David Cinamon, Bruce Anderson, AIA, Nick Reid
Contractor: Charter Construction, Inc.
Structural Engineer: Dave Eisenman, KPFF Consulting Engineers
Photographers: Chris Eden (p. 90), Richard Brown (p. 83 bottom), Art Grice (p. 78, 80, 81, 83 top, 84, 85, 86, 87, 88, 89, 91 middle, bottom), James Cutler Architecs (p. 91 top)

PAULK RESIDENCE; Seabeck, Washington, 1994
Awards: AIA Seattle Honor Award 1994
AIA/Wood Council Merit Award 1995
AIA/Western Red Cedar Excellence Award 1994
AIA/Sunset/Western Homes Award Citation 1995
Client: Elenor and John Paulk
Project Team: Jim Cutler, FAIA, Bruce Anderson, AIA
Contractor: Pleasant Beach Construction
Structural Engineer: Ratti Swenson Perbix
Photographers: Art Grice, Timothy Hursley, reprinted by permission from *House Beautiful*, © July 1996, The Hearst Corporation. All rights reserved (p. 95 bottom, 100 top, 102)

HOUDEK/POPE RESIDENCE; Seabeck, Washington (In Progress)
Client: George Houdek and Myra Pope
Project Team: Jim Cutler, FAIA, Bruce Anderson, AIA
Contractor: Owner
Structural Engineer: Greg Hiatt
Photographer: Art Grice

WATERMAN CABIN; Snake River, Idaho (In Progress)
Client: Gary Waterman
Project Team: Jim Cutler, FAIA, David Cinamon
Contractor: Owner
Photographers: Art Grice, Gary Waterman (p. 111 right)

GUNNELSON CABIN; Ballard Lake, Wisconsin (In Progress)
Client: Jerry Gunnelson
Project Team: Jim Cutler, FAIA, Robert Drucker
Contractor: Owner
Photographer: Jerry Gunnelson

SALEM WITCH TRIALS TERCENTENARY MEMORIAL; Salem, Massachusetts (with Maggie Smith, Artist), 1992
Awards: AIA National Honor Award 1994
AIA Seattle Honor Award 1993
Boston Society of Architects Honor Award 1993
Client: The City of Salem
Project Team: Jim Cutler, FAIA, Maggie Smith, Bruce Anderson, AIA, David Cinamon
Contractor: Hayden Hillsgrove
Landscape Architect: Cynthia Smith and Craig Halvorsen, Halvorsen & Assoc.
Photographers: Steve Rosenthal, Maggie Smith (p. 118 left)
Model Photographer: Paul Lyden (p. 121 top and bottom)

ARMED FORCES MEMORIAL; Norfolk, Virginia (In Progress)
(with Maggie Smith, Artist)
Client: City of Norfolk
Project Team: Jim Cutler, FAIA, Stephen Rising, Aubrey Summers, and Maggie Smith (Artist)
Contractor: to be decided
Structural Engineer: URS Consultants, Inc.
Photographers: Art Grice (p. 125, 128), Lynn Hogan (p. 127), Maggie Smith (p. 124)

ADDITIONAL PHOTOGRAPHIC CREDITS
Jim Cutler (p. 6 left)
Art Grice (p. 6 right, 9 right, 10 top, 11 bottom, 32, 128, 131)
Bruce Anderson (p. 10 bottom)
Peter Aaron/Esto (p. 7, 11 middle, 12)
Jim Parker (p. 9 left, middle)
Karl Backus (p. 11 top)

ACKNOWLEDGMENTS

This book and its contents represent the efforts, thoughts, and support of many people. I would like to thank a few of them.

For the book itself, I would like to thank: Oscar Riera Ojeda, for finding more in our work than we knew was there; Kirsten Jewell, who single-handedly and doggedly assembled, critiqued, correlated, cajoled and willed this book into completion; and Art Grice, for the magnificent photography that he has produced for us for the last fifteen years.

I am deeply grateful to the individuals whose thoughts influenced and formed the beliefs of this office: my Uncle Henry, who taught me to look; Louis Kahn for teaching me how to find the beginning; to the writings of Barry Lopez and Richard Nelson, which awakened feelings I always had; to Peter Bohlin, who, forever, altered my conception of form and who reinforced and validated my beliefs; and to Bruce Anderson, who has been my constant critic and colleague for 13 years.

Finally, I would like to thank my clients for their trust, patience, and perseverance; Pam Cutler, who emotionally supported me for twenty-one years; my departed mother, who taught me how to try; and my father, who taught me how to love.

Dedicated to Dad